Goodhousekeeping Cook's Year

Summer KITCHEN

Good Housekeeping Cook's Year

Summer KITCHEN

DELICIOUS RECIPES AND SEASONAL IDEAS FOR SUMMER COOKING AND ENTERTAINING

EBURY PRESS
LONDON

First published in 1997

1 3 5 7 9 10 8 6 4 2

First published in the United Kingdom in 1997 by Ebury Press
Random House, 20 Vauxhall Bridge Road, London, SW1V 2SA

Random House Australia (Pty) Limited
20 Alfred Street, Milsons Point, Sydney
New South Wales 2061, Australia

Random House New Zealand Limited
18 Poland Road, Glenfield,
Auckland 10, New Zealand

Random House South Africa (Pty) Limited
Endulini, 5a Jubilee Road,
Parktown, 2193, South Africa

Random House UK Limited Reg. No. 954009

A CIP catalogue record for this book is available from the British Library.

ISBN 0 09 185366 4

Managing Editor: Julia Canning
Design: Sara Kidd

Contributing authors: Jacqueline Clark, Maxine Clark, Joanna Farrow, Jane Newdick, Louise Pickford, Louise Steel, Caroline Richmond Walker
Contributing editors: Helen Southall, Donna Wood
Additional research and assistance: Hilary Bird, Fiona Hunter, Sara Lewis
Recipe testing: Emma-Lee Gow, Patricia Stone

Special photography: Ken Field, Michelle Garrett, Graham Kirk
Photgraphic styling: Michelle Garrett, Roisin Nield, Helen Payne
Food for photography: Maxine Clark, Jane Newdick, Louise Pickford, Liz Trigg, Joanna Farrow
Colour illustrations: Madeleine David

Printed and bound in Portugal by Printer Portuguesa, Lisbon

The material in this book was previously published in
Good Housekeeping Cook's Year

Contents

COOKERY NOTES

- Both metric and imperial measures are given for the recipes. Follow either metric or imperial throughout as they are not interchangeable.
- All spoon measures are level unless otherwise stated. Sets of measuring spoons are available in metric and imperial for accurate measurements of small quantities.
- Ovens should be preheated to the temperature specified. Grills should be preheated. The cooking times given in the recipes assume that this has been done.
- Where a stage is specified in brackets under freezing, the dish should be frozen at the end of that stage.
- Size 2 eggs should be used except where otherwise specified.
- Use freshly ground black pepper unless otherwise specified.
- Use fresh rather than dried herbs unless dried herbs are suggested in the recipes.
- Stocks should be freshly made if possible. Alternatively, buy ready-made stocks or use good quality stock cubes.

AT-A-GLANCE SYMBOLS

❄ The recipes can be frozen

◷ The recipes can be prepared and cooked in 30 minutes or under.

♡ The recipe is under 350 calories per portion for main courses and under 200 calories for starters, accompaniments and desserts.

SUMMER IS A WONDERFUL TIME of year for any cook. Not only is there an abundance of glorious fresh produce to choose from, but there is also a wealth of opportunities for easy-going picnics. Food is fresh and light, but also full of the strong, fully-ripened flavours of the season. With summer fruit and fresh salad ingredients at their best, cooking can be simple and quick, allowing the quality of the ingredients to shine through. The pages that follow provide a superb guide for the summer kitchen, with seasonal decorating ideas as well as delicious and imaginative recipes using the best that the season has to offer.

'Summertime and the livin' is easy' goes the song - and how true! The abundance of fresh produce available during the summer months certainly makes cooking easier and the warmer weather inspires a more relaxed attitude to everyday eating and entertaining. This is the season of picnics, barbecues and holiday cooking, all of which should be fun, with the minimum of fuss and preparation.

SUMMER SALADS

The many different varieties of salad leaves now widely available make summer salads a joy to create. Go for different colour combinations and balance soft leaves with a crunchy texture, peppery leaves with sweet. Be brave and experiment!

Salad Combinations

- For a piquant salad, combine one radicchio with a bunch of watercress, a medium frisée, 50 g (2 oz) baby spinach, 50 g (2 oz) rocket and 250 g (9 oz) halved radishes. Fry some small bread croûtons and toss everything together with your favourite dressing.
- For a fruity fennel salad, toss together sliced fennel with orange and grapefruit segments and diced cucumber for added crunch.
- Add 'wild' foods such as sorrel, young dandelion leaves and nasturtium flowers, leaves and seeds.
- Combine traditional salad ingredients like cucumber, Cos or Webb's lettuce with crisply cooked vegetables such as beans, mangetouts, asparagus, baby sweetcorn and broccoli.
- Add seeds - sesame, sunflower - for texture, and roughly chopped walnuts or peanuts for extra crunch.
- Cooked grains, such as couscous and mixed wild rice, make good bases for salads that can be prepared in advance.

A fresh salad of mixed leaves and crisp vegetables, tossed in a herb dressing, epitomizes summer eating.

Dressings

A good dressing will give any salad a lift. A classic vinaigrette is hard to beat and the basic recipe can be varied with different flavourings.

Basic vinaigrette Place 5 ml (1 tsp) Dijon mustard in a screw-top jar with 15 ml (1 tbsp) white wine vinegar, 45-60 ml (3-4 tbsp) olive oil, according to taste, and season with salt and pepper. Shake until well emulsified and use at once.

- For an Italian-style dressing, omit the mustard, add 5 ml (1 tsp) balsamic vinegar, 1 crushed garlic clove and 15 ml (1 tbsp) chopped fresh oregano or parsley.
- Use walnut or hazelnut oil instead of olive oil, but mix with a flavourless oil, such as groundnut or sunflower, to dilute the intensity.
- Use lemon or orange juice instead of vinegar, or try herb, spice or fruit vinegars.
- Try adding 5 ml (1 tsp) pesto sauce or sun-dried tomato paste for a Mediterranean touch. Alternatively, stir in chopped fresh herbs.

TOMATOES

Many different varieties of tomato are now appearing on the supermarket shelves – red and yellow cherry tomatoes, large beef tomatoes, oval Italian plum tomatoes, Provençal tomatoes to mention a few. Unfortunately, many of these are picked too early and as a result can be hard and lacking in flavour.

One way to ripen tomatoes is to set them on a sunny window sill for at least a week - you will notice that the colour deepens and that they become soft and sweet. Leaving the stalks on helps as well. Refrigerate the tomatoes once ripened, but eat quickly.

Here are a few ways to bring out the best in tomatoes.

- Mix 450 g (1 lb) cherry tomatoes with 60 ml (4 tbsp) olive oil, 2 crushed garlic cloves and salt and pepper. Toss to coat, then grill under a hot grill until charred. Serve hot or cold as a tasty accompaniment.
- Plum tomatoes are very firm and are particularly suitable for grilling and roasting as they tend not to

collapse too much.

- Add 4 diced tomatoes to 60 ml (4 tbsp) homemade pesto (see page 11) to make a wonderful light sauce for 350 g (12 oz) cooked pasta.
- Stir halved small tomatoes into hot pasta with a handful of rocket and some soft cheese for a quick summery snack.
- Make a salad using different shaped and coloured tomatoes, arranging the slices on a shallow platter. Spoon over a vinaigrette dressing made with a pinch of sugar and a little chopped mint to bring out the flavour.
- Fill ripe beef tomatoes with a mixture of couscous, toasted pine nuts and chopped roasted peppers for a vegetarian meal.
- Top thick Spanish omelettes with sliced tomatoes, cover with grated cheese and grill – this makes a great supper dish.

FRESH HERBS

Herbs are easy to grow - in the garden, on the patio or even on window sills - and can turn a simple summer dish into something quite memorable! Add chopped fresh herbs to mayonnaise, dressings, sauces and marinades to add extra flavour to meat, fish and vegetables, or use whole sprigs for pretty garnishes. Preserve the fresh flavours in the following ways.

Herb Oils and Vinegars

To capture the flavour of herbs for a short while try making herb oils and vinegars.

Herb oils Here are two simple methods.

- Wash and dry a large bunch of basil leaves and layer them in a flat dish. Cover with about 150 ml (5 fl oz) light olive oil, cover with a clean tea towel and leave in the sun for about 6 hours. Strain the oil into clean jars and keep refrigerated for up to 1 month.
- Blanch a large bunch of coriander, basil or mint leaves and refresh in iced water. Drain and pat dry on absorbent kitchen paper. Place in a blender with 150 ml (5 fl oz) light olive oil and blend until smooth. Pour into a jar and refrigerate overnight. Strain through two layers of muslin without pressing, then decant into clean bottles. Use the precious oil in dressings or just pour neat over salad.

Herb vinegars can be made in the same way as herb oil – or simply add your favourite fresh herb to a bottle of wine or cider vinegar and keep for at least a week.

Herb oils and fruit flavoured vinegars are very easy to make and will lend a subtle taste to salad dressings, sauces and marinades.

Freezing Herbs

A handy way to store chopped fresh herbs is to place them in ice-cube trays, top them with water and freeze. Pop an ice cube or two into a sauce or soup and allow to melt or use as an unusual garnish for chilled soup.

SALMON

Fresh salmon is a summmer favourite. The wild variety is a real treat, but the cheaper farmed version is still prized for its delicate flavour and attractive pink flesh. One of the great advantages of salmon is that it is easy to cook. A whole poached or baked salmon (see page 23) is ideal for a party, but cuts of salmon can provide quick summery dishes that will suit any occasion. Steaks and fillets are the quickest to cook and when marinated only need 30 minutes for the flavours to be absorbed. A large fillet coated with spices is excellent for barbecuing (see recipe page 22) or try brushing salmon steaks with a little soy sauce or teriyaki marinade and grill until charred, basting well.

- A delicate cucumber and dill sauce makes the perfect accompaniment to poached salmon. Peel, deseed and dice a cucumber. Melt 25 g (1 oz) butter, add the cucumber and cook for 2 minutes, then add 150 ml (5 fl oz) dry white wine and boil until all the liquid has disappeared. Stir in 45 ml (3 tbsp) chopped fresh dill or chervil and 60 ml (4 tbsp) crème fraîche, adjust the seasoning and serve at once.

SUMMER SHELLFISH

Fresh crab and crustacea, such as shrimps, langoustine (Dublin Bay prawns), lobster, winkles and so on, are wonderful at this time of year and make a great addition to a seafood platter. Buy the shellfish ready cooked for easy entertaining.

• For a summer seafood feast, present a crab to each guest or a platter of mixed crustacea on a bed of ice, together with crackers and lobster picks, a couple of herby or spicy dips, a few salads and lots of brown bread - and get cracking! Offer plenty of halved lemons for cleaning fingers afterwards.

• Frozen crabmeat is excellent for making the best peppery crab sandwiches - mix light and dark meat together with a little mayonnaise, some Tabasco and plenty of black pepper. Use generously to fill freshly sliced brown bread. Ideal for adding a special touch to picnic food.

SOFT SUMMER FRUITS

Strawberries, raspberries and the various currants are one of the great delights of summer. Delicately flavoured and deliciously juicy, these luscious fruits make wonderful, easy desserts.

• Summer Pudding (see recipe page 62) is a summer classic. A divine combination of mixed red fruit, this pudding is traditionally made with bread, but for a change, try using Madeira sponge instead. Sliced brioche is good too, as is thickly sliced Pannetone. Even a bought flan sponge works well, as the fruit really needs no embellishment. Serve with extra fruit juice and cream whisked with rosewater and a little grated orange rind to enhance the fruity flavours.

Strawberry Ideas

Turn 450 g (1 lb) strawberries into the following quick treats.

• Marinate the halved strawberries and segmented oranges in a couple of tablespoons of Cointreau for 20 minutes and serve with crème fraîche.

• Place whole berries in a bowl. Halve 2 passion fruit, scoop out the pulp and toss with the berries.

• Dip the tips of perfect strawberries into melted white, dark or milk chocolate. Leave on non-stick paper to harden and pile up on a dish decorated with flowers for that special dinner party dessert.

• Halve strawberries and grind over black pepper and a drizzle of balsamic or sherry vinegar - an explosion of flavour and very refreshing!

• Quickly sauté halved berries in butter, adding a little honey and balsamic vinegar and serve immediately with scoops of vanilla ice cream.

• Purée raspberries with a little sugar and kirsch, sieve and pour over halved strawberries.

• For handy sauces, purée strawberries and freeze in ice cube trays for quick thawing. Raspberry purée is a useful standby too.

Fruit Vinegars

It's always worth making jams and jellies from a glut of soft fruit, but why not try making your own fruit vinegars as well. Perfect for adding subtle flavouring to dressings and sauces, fruit vinegars are surprisingly easy to make. Simply place the fruit in a bowl and break it up slightly. For each 450 g (1 lb) soft fruit, pour in 600 ml (1 pint) red or white wine vinegar. Cover with a cloth and leave to stand for 3-4 days, stirring occasionally. Then strain through muslin, measure the vinegar and add 450 g (1 lb) sugar for each 600 ml (1 pint). Boil for 10 minutes then cool. Strain again, pour into bottles and seal with airtight and vinegar-proof tops.

BARBECUES

Barbecues are a great way of making the most of the long summer evenings and are perfect for easy, informal entertaining. Meat and fish, basted with tasty sauces and marinades, are popular barbecue fare, but the plentiful vegetables of summer are equally delicious cooked on the barbecue. Try these simple vegetable ideas for side dishes or a vegetarian feast.

• Slice red onions into 1 cm (½ inch) rounds and slide onto skewers. Barbecue on both sides, brushing with sweet chilli sauce.

• Remove the stem from the base of a large field mushroom, brush with olive oil, lemon juice, salt and pepper. Place on the grill stalk-side down for 1-2 minutes. Turn over and fill the cavity with garlic butter or pesto sauce. Heat for another 1-2 minutes.

• Cook whole ripe tomatoes over a low fire for 1-2 minutes, turning occasionally until soft and lightly charred.

• For minted aubergines, lightly fry 6 sliced garlic cloves in 15 ml (1 tbsp) olive oil. Add 180 ml (12 tbsp) wine vinegar and 60 ml (4 tbsp) sugar. Heat slowly until the sugar dissolves and reduce by half.

Barbecue a selection of summer vegetables alongside succulent pieces of meat or fish to create a complete al fresco feast, full of delicious smoky flavours.

Add 90 ml (6 tbsp) roughly chopped fresh mint. Drizzle over 450 g (1 lb) sliced grilled aubergines. Serve hot or cold.

• Halve or quarter chicory or radicchio, leaving the core in place. Grill on a cool part of the barbecue, turning frequently until beginning to wilt, then drizzle with olive oil and reduced balsamic vinegar. (To make reduced vinegar, boil balsamic vinegar in a pan until reduced by half - keep in a jar and use sparingly.)

Finishing Touches

Marinades and accompanying dips and sauces can make all the difference to the flavour of barbecued food.

Watercress pesto Put 75 g (3 oz) soft goats' cheese in a blender or food processor with 25 g (1 oz) Gruyère cheese, 200 ml (7 fl oz) olive oil, 25 g (1 oz) pistachio nuts, 1 garlic clove, 2.5 ml (1/2 tsp) salt and 75 g (3 oz) watercress and blend until smooth. Serve with barbecued or grilled steak or fish, or spoon over baked potatoes.

Basil aioli Blend 175 ml (6 fl oz) olive oil with 125 g (4 oz) fresh basil in a blender or food processor, then transfer to a jug. Blend 1 egg yolk with 15 ml (1 tbsp) white wine vinegar and half the basil oil. Blend together until thickening, then add 1 garlic clove and the remaining basil oil. Work for 30 seconds and season. Use as a dip for barbecued vegetables.

Spiced marinade Mix 150 ml (5 fl oz) soy sauce with 150 ml (5 fl oz) dry or medium sherry, 4 garlic cloves, 2.5 cm (1 inch) grated fresh ginger root, 30 ml (2 tbsp) clear honey, 2.5 ml (1/2 tsp) ground star anise and 30 ml (2 tbsp) chopped fresh coriander. Use for marinating lamb, chicken pieces or a whole salmon.

Sun-dried tomato butter Blend in a food processor 1 small bunch chives, 25 g (1 oz) pitted black olives, 30 ml (2 tbsp) sun-dried tomato paste, 225 g (8oz) softened unsalted butter, 1 garlic clove and black pepper. Use to top barbecued food.

HERB FRAME

The plentiful fresh herbs of summer have innumerable uses in the kitchen, but their delicate colouring and attractive aroma also make them ideal for decorative purposes. A rich harvest of herbs can be turned into a subtle, sweet-smelling display that will enhance any summer setting.

Here a simple wooden structure is covered with bunches of mixed herbs to create a fresh, leafy frame that will add a touch of natural colour and scent to a room. Hang or prop the frame against a plain wall for a simple, rustic look, or use the frame flat as part of a table setting - herb displays look particularly good set against crisp, white table linen and wrought iron candle holders.

You will need:
Twelve 40 cm (16 inch) lengths and four 10 cm (4 inch) lengths of garden training wood
Garden string
Scissors
Florist's wire on a reel
Large bunches of fresh herbs, such as rosemary sage, oregano, lavender
Ribbon with wire edging

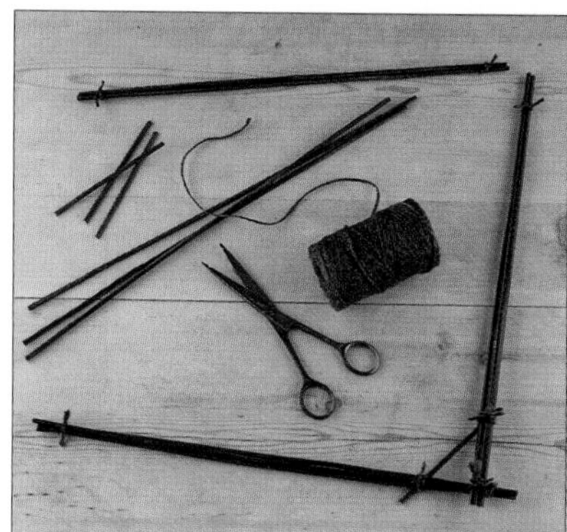

1 Bind together three 40 cm (16 inch) lengths of wood by tying with string 2.5 cm (1 inch) in from either end. Repeat with remaining 40 cm (16 inch) wood to make the four sides of the frame. Arrange into a square frame shape, overlapping the wood at the knots, then tie in place. To give extra support, attach a 10 cm (4 inch) length of wood across each corner.
2 Separate the herbs into sprigs and trim to 10-15 cm (4-6 inch) lengths. Tie into small bunches, using 4-6 mixed sprigs per bunch.

3 Lay one bunch along the wooden frame, positioning the stems at a slight angle. Bind the bunch in place with wire, winding it around two or three times. Do not cut the wire. Place another bunch on the frame at a different angle, close enough to cover the stems of first bunch. Bind as before.
4 Continue binding on bunches until the frame is completely covered in herbs. Finish with a ribbon bow.
5 Move the completed frame with care, as the structure is fairly delicate.

ROSE RIBBONS

Ribbons of rose buds are a wonderfully romantic idea, suited to the most glamorous occasions such as a wedding or a landmark anniversary. Threaded onto fine florist's wire, the rose buds can be used to spell out initials on the table. For a more flexible ribbon, use thread instead of wire - try looping this around the edge of a buffet table, catching it in places with a large rose.

Experiment with different flowers and buds. To save money, you can alternate roses with leaves and fresh flowers from the garden.

You will need:
Plenty of the smallest rose buds available
Fine florist's wire
Fine strong thread
Darning needle

1 For a wired rose 'ribbon', simply push a length of wire across the base of a bud or up through the bud and out at the top. Continue threading buds along the wire until the 'ribbon' is as long as required.

2 To form initials, trace out the letters on a piece of paper first, enlarging them from a pattern book if necessary. Bend the rose ribbon round the traced pattern then slide the paper out.

3 For a looser rose 'ribbon' string buds onto thread with a darning needle to form a long chain of roses.

4 Wrap the chain of rose buds around dishes, loop it along the edge of a table or twist it around glass stems.

MELON FLOWER BOWL

A carved melon bowl filled with brightly-coloured flowers is the perfect finishing touch for a summer table setting. Creating the decorative edge of the melon is easy, yet very effective, and the scooped-out shell makes an excellent holder. If wished, use the melon as part of the meal, perhaps as a starter filled with salad and topped with edible flowers, such as nasturtiums.

The sculptured look of this display can be enhanced by adding other carved fruit to the setting - for instance, the skin of a whole pomelo or other large citrus fruit can be given a dramatic pattern by simply carving into the rind with a zester or peeler.

You will need:
1 melon, such as ogen or charentais
Large sharp knife
Small sharp knife
Dessert spoon
Edible flowers and leaves, such as geraniums
Side plate

1 Using a large knife, cut a thin slice off the bottom of the melon so that it stands upright.

2 Using a small sharp knife, cut round the top third of the melon in a zig-zag pattern. Remove top from melon.

3 Scoop out the seeds from the centre of the melon with a dessert spoon.

4 Arrange stems of flowers and leaves in the scooped-out melon and stand on a small plate to create an attractive display.

ICED BOTTLES

Frosted bottles look spectacular encased in ice with flowers, leaves and fruits trapped in it. This attractive idea only works for bottles filled with spirits, such as schnapps and vodka, that have a low freezing point. However, strong empty bottles can also be packed in ice and used to serve drinks at a summer party or barbecue – a perfect way of keeping drinks cool! Stand the iced-up bottles on a tray or plate to catch the drips as they slowly melt.

Large milk containers with their tops cut off make ideal moulds in which to freeze the bottles. The containers and bottles take up a fair amount of space in the freezer, so make room in advance. Carefully build up the ice in layers to distribute the flowers and fruit evenly throughout. Spring water is less likely than tap water to freeze cloudy.

You will need:
Vodka, schnapps or flavoured vodka in strong bottles
Plastic milk containers for moulds
Spring water or tap water
Flowers, petals and leaves
Fruits, such as cherries, strawberries

1 Cut off the top of the plastic container horizontally and make space in the freezer to stand it upright. Pour 2.5 cm (1 inch) water into the base and place in the freezer until frozen solid.

2 Stand the bottle centrally in the container and add another 2.5 cm (1 inch) water. If the bottle moves around, wedge it with paper or wooden skewers near the top, above the water level. Place in the freezer again to freeze until the bottle is firmly anchored.

3 Arrange flowers, leaves and fruit around the bottle and pour in 10 cm (4 inches) water. Leave to freeze and continue building up in layers until the container is full.

4 When the last layer of water is frozen, take the container out of the freezer and plunge it briefly into a deep bowl or sinkful of hot water. The plastic container should slide off easily. Return the frozen bottle to the freezer until it is needed.

CHILLED TOMATO AND VODKA SOUP

PREPARATION TIME 10 minutes plus chilling
FREEZING Not suitable
♡

SERVES 6

55 CALS/SERVING

- *125 g (4 oz) celery, trimmed and chopped*
- *1 red pepper, deseeded and chopped*
- *900 ml (1½ pints) tomato juice*
- *60 ml (4 tbsp) vodka*
- *45 ml (3 tbsp) chopped fresh coriander*
- *60 ml (4 tbsp) Worcestershire sauce*
- *juice of 2 lemons, about 45 ml (3 tbsp)*
- *2.5 ml (½ tsp) chilli sauce*
- *salt and pepper*
- *3 garlic cloves, peeled and crushed*
- *crushed ice, to serve (optional)*

1 Mix the celery and pepper with the remaining ingredients in a large bowl.
2 Cover and chill for at least 1 hour. Serve over a little crushed ice, if wished.

CHILLED AVOCADO AND LIME SOUP

PREPARATION TIME 5-10 minutes, plus chilling
COOKING TIME 15-20 minutes
FREEZING Not suitable

SERVES 4

235 CALS/SERVING

- *15 ml (1 tbsp) extra-virgin olive oil*
- *1 bunch spring onions, trimmed and sliced*
- *225 g (8 oz) potatoes, peeled and cubed*
- *900 ml (1½ pints) vegetable stock*
- *1-2 limes*
- *2 ripe avocados*
- *salt and pepper*
- *90 ml (6 tbsp) very low-fat fromage frais*
- *snipped chives, to garnish*

1 Heat the oil in a large saucepan, add the spring onions and fry gently until softened.
2 Add the potato to the softened onions and fry, stirring, for 2 minutes. Add the stock and bring to the boil. Cover and simmer for 15-20 minutes.
3 Towards the end of the cooking time, remove a little zest from one of the limes, using a zester, and set aside for the garnish. Squeeze the juice from the lime. Halve, stone and peel the avocados, then chop roughly. Add the avocado to the soup with the lime juice. Taste and adjust the seasoning; add extra lime juice (from the other lime) if required.
4 Remove the soup from the heat, allow to cool slightly, then work until smooth in a blender or food processor. Add 30 ml (2 tbsp) fromage frais and stir to mix. Pour into soup bowls and chill for 3-4 hours. (The soup thickens as it is chilled.)
5 To serve, add a swirl of fromage frais and a squeeze of lime juice. Grind some black pepper on top and garnish with snipped chives and the lime zest. Serve with Melba Toast.

TIP

To make Melba Toast, cut 4-5 thin slices from a day-old loaf of wholemeal bread. Toast lightly on both sides. Quickly cut off the crusts and split each slice in two horizontally. Bake in a 180°C (350°F) mark 4 oven for 10-15 minutes until crisp and curled.

LETTUCE AND SORREL SOUP

PREPARATION TIME 15 minutes
COOKING TIME 20-25 minutes
FREEZING Suitable
❄

SERVES 4
- *60 ml (4 tbsp) extra-virgin olive oil*
- *6 spring onions, chopped*
- *1 garlic clove, peeled and crushed*
- *5 ml (1 tsp) chopped fresh thyme (lemon thyme preferably)*
- *50 g (2 oz) long-grain rice*
- *450 g (1 lb) cos lettuce, shredded*

205 CALS/SERVING
- *125 g (4 oz) sorrel, shredded*
- *1.2 litres (2 pints) vegetable stock*
- *30 ml (2 tbsp) chopped fresh chives*
- *pinch of grated nutmeg*
- *salt and pepper*
- *Parmesan cheese shavings, to garnish (optional)*

1 Heat 15 ml (1 tbsp) of the oil in a saucepan, add the spring onions, garlic and thyme and fry gently for 5 minutes until softened but not coloured. Add the rice and stir-fry for 1 minute.
2 Stir in the lettuce and the sorrel and pour in the stock. Bring to the boil, cover and simmer gently for 15 minutes until the rice is cooked.
3 Transfer to a blender or food processor, add the chives and nutmeg and purée until smooth. Return the soup to the pan, and heat through, whisking in the remaining oil and seasoning with salt and pepper. Serve hot, garnished with a little Parmesan.

VARIATIONS For a more substantial soup, omit the rice, reduce the lettuce to 225 g (8 oz) and add 225 g (8 oz) potatoes. If sorrel is not available, use spinach instead.

SPICY CRAB DIP

PREPARATION TIME 10 minutes, plus chilling
FREEZING Not suitable
♡

SERVES 4
- *225 g (8 oz) white crab meat, flaked*
- *225 g (8 oz) soft cheese*
- *45 ml (3 tbsp) canned pimiento, finely chopped*
- *juice of ½ lemon*

135 CALS/SERVING
- *10 ml (2 tsp) Worcestershire sauce*
- *5 ml (1 tsp) anchovy essence*
- *1.25 ml (¼ tsp) cayenne pepper*
- *salt and pepper*
- *crudités, to serve*

1 Fold the crab meat into the soft cheese until evenly mixed.
2 Fold in the pimiento, then stir in the lemon juice, Worcestershire sauce, anchovy essence and cayenne and season with salt and pepper. Turn into a serving bowl and chill for at least 2 hours. Serve with crudités.

BRUSCHETTA

PREPARATION TIME 20 minutes
COOKING TIME 4 minutes
FREEZING Not suitable
◴

SERVES 6
- *12 slices Italian bread (such as Ciabatta), about 2 cm (¾ inch) thick*
- *salt and pepper*
- *1-2 garlic cloves, peeled*
- *90 ml (6 tbsp) olive oil*
- *lemon rind and basil leaves, to garnish*

HERB AND LEMON TOPPING
- *15 ml (1 tbsp) each chopped fresh mint and parsley*
- *15 ml (1 tbsp) lemon juice*

300 CALS/SERVING

TOMATO TOPPING
- *3 plum or very ripe tomatoes, skinned, deseeded and diced*
- *15 ml (1 tbsp) pesto sauce*
- *30 ml (2 tbsp) chopped fresh basil*

TAPENADE TOPPING
- *45-60 ml (3-4 tbsp) tapenade (black olive paste)*
- *4 pitted black olives, shredded*

1 To make the toppings, mix together the ingredients in three small separate bowls and season each with salt and pepper to taste.
2 Toast both sides of the slices of bread until golden. Press the garlic cloves with the blade of a large knife to bruise them and rub over one side of each slice. Drizzle the toast with olive oil, then spoon each of the toppings onto four of the slices.
3 Drizzle the remaining olive oil on top and garnish the Herb and Lemon Topping with lemon rind and the Tomato Topping with basil leaves. Serve while still hot and crisp.

SKEWERED TIGER PRAWNS WITH PARMA HAM

PREPARATION TIME 20 minutes, plus marinating
COOKING TIME 4-6 minutes
FREEZING Not suitable
♡

SERVES 4

- *225 g (8 oz) raw tiger prawns*
- *65 g (2½ oz) sliced Parma ham*
- *coriander or flat-leaf parsley sprigs, to garnish*

MARINADE

- *1 shallot, peeled and finely chopped*
- *1 garlic clove, peeled and crushed*

200 CALS/SERVING

- *5 ml (1 tsp) wholegrain mustard*
- *1 small fresh red chilli, deseeded and very finely sliced*
- *15 ml (1 tbsp) olive oil*
- *juice of ½ lemon*
- *salt and pepper*

1 Peel the prawns, discarding the heads. Cut down the back of each prawn and remove the black intestinal vein. Wash and dry well. Thread the prawns onto 8 small bamboo skewers which have been previously soaked in warm water for 30 minutes.
2 Cut the Parma ham slices in half lengthways and wrap around the skewered prawns. Place the skewers in a glass or china dish and set aside.
3 Mix together the marinade ingredients and pour over the skewered prawns. Cover and marinate in the refrigerator for 1-2 hours, turning occasionally.
4 Drain the skewered prawns and place on a grill rack. Cook under a hot grill for 4-6 minutes, basting with the marinade and turning occasionally until the prawns are cooked and the ham is beginning to crisp and brown. Serve at once, garnished with coriander or parsley sprigs.

VARIATION Thread lemon wedges onto the skewers, in between the prawns.

SPINACH, BACON AND ROQUEFORT SALAD

PREPARATION TIME 15 minutes
COOKING TIME 10 minutes
FREEZING Not suitable
◴

SERVES 8
- *8 slices French bread, cut on the diagonal into slices about 2.5 cm (1 inch) thick*
- *120 ml (8 tbsp) olive oil*
- *175 g (6 oz) streaky bacon or pancetta (Italian bacon), sliced very thinly*
- *50 g (2 oz) pine nuts*
- *60 ml (4 tbsp) sesame oil*

520 CALS/SERVING
- *30 ml (2 tbsp) red wine vinegar*
- *pepper*
- *125 g (4 oz) baby spinach, washed*
- *125 g (4 oz) Roquefort cheese, crumbled*
- *175 g (6 oz) black seedless grapes, halved*

1 Brush both sides of each slice of French bread with 60 ml (4 tbsp) of the olive oil. Place on a baking sheet. Halve or chop the bacon and place on a second baking sheet with the pine nuts. Cook at 230°C (450°F) mark 8 for about 10 minutes or until the bread slices are golden brown and the bacon is cooked, turning all the food halfway through.
2 Whisk the remaining 60 ml (4 tbsp) olive oil with the sesame oil, vinegar and pepper.
3 Pile the spinach, bacon, cheese, pine nuts and grapes on the croûtes. Pour on the dressing and toss well.

COURGETTE AND PESTO ROUNDS

PREPARATION TIME 20 minutes
COOKING TIME 10 minutes
FREEZING Not suitable
♡ ◴

SERVES 6
- *225 g (8 oz) courgettes*
- *olive oil*
- *2 beefsteak tomatoes, about 450 g (1 lb) total weight*
- *30 ml (2 tbsp) red pesto sauce or tapenade (black olive paste)*

90 CALS/SERVING
- *large handful of fresh basil leaves*
- *salt and pepper*
- *50 g (2 oz) fresh Parmesan cheese*

1 Cut the courgettes diagonally into slices about 5 mm (¼ inch) thick. Lightly brush a non-stick frying pan with oil. Cook the courgette slices on both sides for about 5 minutes or until brown and tender.
2 Cut each tomato into 3 slices about 1 cm (½ inch) thick and place on a lightly oiled baking sheet. Spread 5 ml (1 tsp) of pesto or tapenade on top of each slice. Place 5 or 6 basil leaves in a circle on top of the pesto.
3 Place an overlapping circle of courgettes on the basil leaves. Season with salt and pepper.
4 Cook at 200°C (400°F) mark 6 for 10 minutes. Top with thinly pared Parmesan cheese. Serve immediately.

VARIATION ***Courgette and Mozzarella Rounds***
This recipe works equally well with mozzarella cheese. Assemble the rounds as above but top each one with a thin slice of mozzarella at the end of stage 3 – you'll need about 75 g (3 oz). Cook as directed in the recipe above, then brown under a hot grill before serving.

CUCUMBER AND STRAWBERRY SALAD

PREPARATION TIME 40 minutes
FREEZING Not suitable
♡

SERVES 4
- *½ cucumber*
- *salt and pepper*
- *225 g (8 oz) ripe strawberries*
- *2 fresh ripe figs, wiped*

130 CALS/SERVING
- *45 ml (3 tbsp) sunflower oil*
- *15 ml (1 tbsp) balsamic or wine vinegar*

1 Score the skin of the cucumber lengthways with the prongs of a fork. Slice the cucumber very thinly, then place on a plate and sprinkle with salt. Leave to stand for about 30 minutes to draw out the excess moisture.
2 Meanwhile, prepare the strawberries and figs. Reserve a few small strawberries for the garnish. Slice the remaining strawberries in half lengthways. Slice the figs into quarters lengthways.
3 To prepare the dressing, whisk together the oil, vinegar and pepper with a fork.
4 Drain the cucumber and pat dry with absorbent kitchen paper. Arrange the cucumber slices, quartered figs and halved strawberries on a serving plate. Sprinkle over the dressing, then garnish with the reserved whole strawberries. Serve as soon as possible.

TIP
The combination of sweet and sour in this salad is unusual, but most refreshing. Do not use malt vinegar as it is too strong. Balsamic vinegar is perfect, or you can use wine vinegar.

MANGO AND PRAWN SALADS

PREPARATION TIME 20 minutes
FREEZING Not suitable
♡ ◷

SERVES 4
- *2 ripe mangoes*
- *225 g (8 oz) cooked, peeled prawns*
- *90 ml (6 tbsp) fromage frais*
- *30 ml (2 tbsp) mayonnaise*
- *grated rind of 1 lime*
- *10 ml (2 tsp) lime juice*

180 CALS/SERVING
- *5 ml (1 tsp) snipped fresh chives*
- *salt and pepper*
- *mixed salad leaves*
- *cooked prawns with their shells on*
- *slices of ripe mango, to garnish*

1 Slice each mango twice lengthways, either side of the stone. Cut the flesh in the segments lengthways and widthways without breaking the skin, then push the skin inside out to expose the cubes of flesh. Slice off and remove the flesh in neat cubes and put in a bowl. Peel the remaining centre sections and cut the flesh away from the stones into cubes. Add to the bowl.
2 Add the peeled prawns, fromage frais, mayonnaise, lime rind and juice, chives, salt and pepper, and mix together.
3 Arrange the mixture on a bed of salad leaves on individual serving plates. Serve garnished with the whole prawns and mango slices.

VARIATION *Melon and Prawn Salads* Replace the mango with a sweet-flavoured melon such as charentais.

SPICED BARBECUED SALMON

PREPARATION TIME 15 minutes
COOKING TIME 15 minutes
FREEZING Not suitable
♡ ◷

SERVES 6

295 CALS/SERVING

- *900 g (2 lb) salmon fillet, with skin on and scales removed*
- *6 cardamom pods*
- *5 ml (1 tsp) cumin seeds*
- *5 ml (1 tsp) coriander seeds*
- *2.5 ml (½ tsp) black peppercorns*
- *2.5 ml (½ tsp) coarse salt*
- *30 ml (2 tbsp) olive oil*

1 Remove any remaining salmon bones with tweezers. Using a sharp knife, slash the skin side into diamonds.
2 Remove the dark seeds from the cardamom pods and discard the pods. Finely grind the seeds with the cumin seeds, coriander seeds, peppercorns and coarse salt in a grinder or with a pestle and mortar.
3 Brush the salmon with the oil and press the spices firmly onto the skin side. Place the salmon in a fish griller and cook on the barbecue for 10-15 minutes, turning halfway through, until brown and crisp but just cooked on the inside.

VARIATIONS The fish can be cooked in the oven, if wished. Place the salmon on an oiled baking sheet and cook at 230°C (450°F) mark 8 for 10-15 minutes.

For an unusual touch, dip a small bunch of mixed herbs into a bowl of olive oil and brush lightly over the fish as it cooks.

TIP
If you barbecue fish frequently it's a good idea to invest in a fish grill, which encloses the fish and makes it much easier to handle.

BAKED SALMON WITH WALNUT OIL AND HERBS

PREPARATION TIME 35 minutes, plus marinating
COOKING TIME 15-20 minutes
FREEZING Not suitable

SERVES 4

490 CALS/SERVING

- *575 g (1¼ lb) salmon fillet, skinned*
- *125 ml (4 fl oz) white wine*
- *50 ml (2 fl oz) walnut oil*
- *60 ml (4 tbsp) chopped fresh mixed herbs, such as parsley and chives*
- *2 garlic cloves, peeled and crushed*
- *large pinch of paprika*
- *salt and pepper*
- *4 sticks celery, cut into matchsticks*
- *225 g (8 oz) young turnips, peeled and cut into matchsticks*
- *olive oil*
- *90 ml (6 tbsp) double cream*
- *lime juice to taste*
- *cooked shrimps or prawns, to garnish*

1 Cut the fillet into four even-size pieces and place in a shallow non-metallic dish. Mix the wine, walnut oil, herbs, garlic, paprika and seasoning. Spoon the mixture over the fish, cover and chill in the refrigerator for at least 4 hours or overnight, turning occasionally.
2 Meanwhile, blanch the celery and turnips together in boiling, salted water for 1 minute, then drain under cold water to cool quickly.
3 Lightly oil a shallow ovenproof dish. Place the celery and turnips in it in a single layer and season well. Lift the salmon out of the marinade and place on top of the vegetables. Reserve the marinade.
4 Bake the salmon and vegetables at 220°C (425°F) mark 7 for 15-20 minutes or until the fish is cooked.
5 Meanwhile, place the marinade and the cream in a small saucepan and boil until reduced by about half. Off the heat, quickly whisk in the lime juice to taste and season with salt and pepper.
6 To serve, arrange the salmon and vegetables on individual serving plates. Spoon the sauce over the top and garnish with shrimps or prawns.

SALMON TROUT WITH HERB SAUCE

PREPARATION TIME 25 minutes, plus cooling
COOKING TIME 40 minutes
FREEZING Not suitable

SERVES 4

- *1 salmon or sea trout, about 900 g (2 lb), cleaned*
- *45 ml (3 tbsp) lemon juice*
- *50 g (2 oz) butter or margarine*
- *salt and pepper*
- *1 bunch watercress, roughly chopped*
- *125 g (4 oz) spinach leaves, roughly chopped*

575 CALS/SERVING

- *45 ml (3 tbsp) chopped fresh parsley*
- *30 ml (2 tbsp) chopped fresh chervil*
- *5 ml (1 tsp) chopped fresh dill*
- *150 ml (5 fl oz) mayonnaise*
- *herb sprigs and lemon rind shapes, to garnish*

1 Place the fish in the centre of a large piece of foil. Add 30 ml (2 tbsp) of the lemon juice, then dot with 25 g (1 oz) of the butter. Season with salt and pepper.

2 Seal the foil, weigh the fish and place on a baking sheet. Calculate the cooking time at 15 minutes per 450 g (1 lb), plus 10 minutes. Bake at 180°C (350°F) mark 4 until tender.

3 Remove the fish from the foil, reserving the cooking liquor, then carefully remove the skin while still warm. Place the fish on a serving dish and leave to cool.

4 To make the sauce, put the cooking liquor and the remaining 25 g (1 oz) butter in a saucepan and heat gently. Add the watercress, spinach, parsley, chervil and dill, then cook for 2-3 minutes or until softened.

5 Put the sauce in a blender or food processor and blend until smooth. Transfer to a bowl, add the remaining lemon juice and season to taste. Leave to cool, then fold in the mayonnaise. Turn into a small serving jug and refrigerate until required.

6 Garnish the fish decoratively with herbs and lemon rind shapes, and serve with the herb sauce.

TUNA STEAKS WITH PARMESAN BASIL BUTTER

PREPARATION TIME 20 minutes, plus marinating
COOKING TIME 12-15 minutes
FREEZING Not suitable

SERVES 6

500 CALS/SERVING

- *6 tuna steaks, cut 2 cm (¾ inch) thick, each weighing about 175 g (6 oz)*
- *fresh herbs, to garnish*

MARINADE

- *100 ml (3½ fl oz) olive oil*
- *2 garlic cloves, peeled and crushed*
- *10 ml (2 tsp) balsamic or sherry vinegar*
- *30 ml (2 tbsp) chopped fresh mixed herbs, such as thyme and parsley*
- *salt and pepper*

PARMESAN BASIL BUTTER

- *75 g (3 oz) unsalted butter, softened*
- *30 ml (2 tbsp) freshly grated Parmesan cheese*
- *5 ml (1 tsp) balsamic or sherry vinegar*
- *5-6 fresh basil leaves*

1 Rinse the steaks and pat dry on absorbent kitchen paper. Place in a shallow non-metallic dish.
2 Whisk together all the marinade ingredients and pour over the steaks. Turn to coat, cover and leave to marinate in the refrigerator for 3-4 hours or overnight.
3 To make the basil butter, beat the butter until soft and creamy. Beat in the Parmesan cheese, vinegar and pepper to taste. Finely shred the basil and stir it into the butter mixture. Spoon into a sausage shape on wet non-stick baking parchment and roll up neatly. Chill for at least 1 hour or until firm enough to slice.
4 Lift the steaks out of the marinade and place directly over the barbecue or under the grill. Cook for 12-15 minutes or until firm and tender, turning once and brushing occasionally with the marinade. The flesh will turn a lighter colour when cooked. Pierce the centre with the tip of a sharp knife to see if it is cooked in the middle.
5 Serve the steaks topped with slices of Parmesan basil butter and garnished with fresh herbs.

VARIATION Use salmon for this dish if fresh tuna is not available.

GRILLED SARDINES WITH TOMATO SAUCE

PREPARATION TIME 20 minutes
COOKING TIME About 20 minutes
FREEZING Not suitable
♡

SERVES 4

295 CALS/SERVING

- *16 small or 8 large sardines, cleaned*
- *30 ml (2 tbsp) olive oil*
- *few sprigs of thyme*
- *pepper*
- *juice of ½ lemon*
- *lemon rind shreds, to garnish*

TOMATO SAUCE

- *15 ml (1 tbsp) olive oil*
- *1 small onion, peeled and finely chopped*
- *1 garlic clove, peeled and finely chopped*
- *450 g (1 lb) ripe tomatoes, finely chopped*
- *15 ml (1 tbsp) chopped fresh parsley*
- *salt and pepper*

1 To make the tomato sauce, heat the oil in a frying pan, add the onion and garlic and fry gently until the onion is softened. Add the tomatoes and parsley, then season with salt and pepper to taste. Cook, uncovered, for 10-15 minutes until the tomatoes are just tender.
2 Meanwhile, score the fish with three or four diagonal cuts on each side. Brush with oil, and push a few sprigs of thyme into some of the cuts. Season with pepper and sprinkle with lemon juice.
3 Arrange the fish on a grill rack and grill for about 4 minutes on each side or until cooked, brushing frequently with the oil and juices.
4 Arrange the sardines on a platter, and pour over any juices from the grill pan. Garnish with lemon rind shreds, and serve with the tomato sauce.

NOTE The sardines can be barbecued, if wished. The sauce can be kept hot on the edge of the barbecue grid.

SPICED FISH KEBABS WITH AVOCADO SALSA

PREPARATION TIME 15 minutes, plus marinating
COOKING TIME 6-8 minutes
FREEZING Not suitable

SERVES 4-6

465-310 CALS/SERVING

- *700 g (1½ lb) monkfish fillets, skinned*
- *12 large raw tiger prawns*

MARINADE

- *2 garlic cloves, peeled and crushed*
- *5 ml (1 tsp) ground coriander*
- *5 ml (1 tsp) ground turmeric*
- *2.5 ml (½ tsp) ground cumin*
- *2.5 ml (½ tsp) sea salt*
- *2.5 ml (½ tsp) chilli powder*
- *1.25 ml (¼ tsp) ground cinnamon*
- *juice of 1 lime*
- *15 ml (1 tbsp) tomato purée*
- *90 ml (6 tbsp) olive oil*

AVOCADO SALSA

- *1 small ripe avocado*
- *½ small red onion, peeled and finely chopped*
- *15 ml (1 tbsp) lime juice*
- *15 ml (1 tbsp) chopped fresh coriander*
- *1 garlic clove, peeled and crushed*
- *pinch of sugar*
- *salt and pepper*

1 Wash and dry the monkfish and cut into 12 large chunks. Peel the prawns, discarding the heads, then cut down the back of each prawn and remove the black intestinal vein. Wash and dry well. Thread the monkfish and prawns alternately onto 4 skewers. Set aside.
2 To make the marinade, combine all the ingredients in a small bowl. Brush the marinade over the kebabs, then transfer to a shallow non-metallic dish, cover and marinate overnight.
3 Remove the kebabs from the refrigerator at least 1 hour before cooking.
4 Just before cooking the kebabs, make the salsa. Stone, peel and dice the avocado, then mix with the onion, lime juice, coriander, garlic and sugar. Season to taste and set aside for 10 minutes.
5 Place the kebabs on an oiled grill pan and grill as close to the heat as possible for 6-8 minutes, turning and basting frequently with the marinade juices, until charred and cooked through. Serve immediately with the salsa.

VARIATION Use any firm fleshed fish for this dish, such as swordfish or tuna. Scallops also work well as an alternative to the prawns.

TIP

If using wooden skewers, soak them in water for 30 minutes before threading on the seafood.

GRILLED HALIBUT WITH STIR-FRIED VEGETABLES

PREPARATION TIME 15 minutes
COOKING TIME 6-10 minutes
FREEZING Not suitable
♡ ◴

SERVES 4

- *4 halibut steaks*
- *melted butter for basting*
- *15 ml (1 tbsp) oil*
- *25 g (1 oz) butter*
- *1 large courgette, cut into matchstick strips*
- *1 red pepper, deseeded and cut into matchstick strips*

280 CALS/SERVING

- *15 ml (1 tbsp) sun-dried tomato paste*
- *10 ml (2 tsp) chopped fresh thyme*
- *10 ml (2 tsp) chopped fresh tarragon or chervil*
- *salt and pepper*
- *tarragon or chervil sprigs, to garnish*

1 Brush the halibut steaks with a little melted butter and grill for about 3-5 minutes on each side or until cooked through.

2 Meanwhile, heat the oil and butter in a frying pan and stir-fry the courgette and pepper strips for about 2 minutes. Stir in the sun-dried tomato paste and chopped herbs, then season with salt and pepper.

3 Serve the halibut with the stir-fried vegetables, garnished with sprigs of herbs.

FRESH SEAFOOD STEW

PREPARATION TIME 30 minutes
COOKING TIME 40 minutes
FREEZING Not suitable
♡

SERVES 6

- *60 ml (4 tbsp) olive oil*
- *900 g (2 lb) onions, peeled and finely sliced*
- *450 g (1 lb) thick cod fillets, skinned and cut into 5 cm (2 inch) pieces*
- *225 g (8 oz) plaice fillets, skinned and quartered*
- *175 g (6 oz) peeled raw tiger prawns*
- *salt and pepper*
- *450 g (1 lb) plum tomatoes, skinned, deseeded and chopped*

335 CALS/SERVING

- *30 ml (2 tbsp) tomato purée*
- *60 ml (4 tbsp) chopped fresh parsley*
- *30 ml (2 tbsp) chopped fresh marjoram or oregano*
- *150 ml (5 fl oz) dry white wine*
- *225 g (8 oz) cooked mixed seafood*
- *oregano leaves, to garnish*

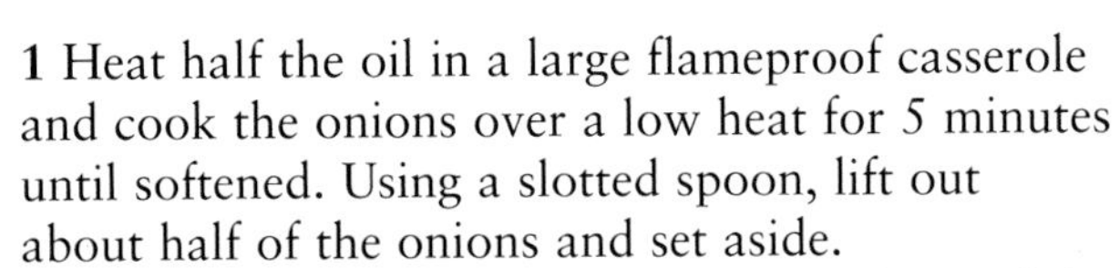

1 Heat half the oil in a large flameproof casserole and cook the onions over a low heat for 5 minutes until softened. Using a slotted spoon, lift out about half of the onions and set aside.
2 Spread the remainder evenly over the base of the casserole, then cover with half the fish and prawns – do not add any of the mixed seafood yet. Season well with salt and pepper to taste.
3 Cover with half of the tomatoes and the tomato purée, then repeat the layers. Sprinkle the herbs on top and pour the wine over. Drizzle the remaining oil on top and cook, uncovered, over a very low heat for about 30 minutes or until the liquid has thickened slightly. Stir in the mixed seafood and heat through for 3-5 minutes. Serve garnished with oregano leaves.

CHILLIED MEDITERRANEAN PRAWNS

PREPARATION TIME 10 minutes
COOKING TIME 5-10 minutes
FREEZING Not suitable
♡ ◷

SERVES 2

- *15 ml (1 tbsp) olive oil*
- *1 garlic clove, peeled and crushed*
- *4 small tomatoes, skinned and chopped*
- *1 fresh medium chilli, deseeded and chopped*

235 CALS/SERVING

- *few drops of Tabasco sauce*
- *salt and pepper*
- *12 raw peeled tiger prawns*
- *slices of lemon, to garnish*

1 Heat the oil in a small frying pan and add the garlic, tomatoes, chilli, a few drops of Tabasco and salt and pepper. Cover and cook gently for about 5 minutes or until the tomatoes are reduced to a pulp.
2 Stir in the prawns and cook gently for about 3 minutes until the prawns are cooked. Garnish with lemon slices.

GRILLED LOBSTER

PREPARATION TIME 20 minutes
COOKING TIME 5 minutes
FREEZING Not suitable
♡ ◴

SERVES 4

- *4 cooked lobsters, each weighing 450-550 g (1-1¼ lb)*
- *salt and pepper*
- *50 g (2 oz) butter,*

305 CALS/SERVING

- *lemon slices and parsley sprigs, to garnish*

1 Twist off the lobster claws and pincers. Crack open the large claws using the back of a heavy knife, being careful not to crush the meat inside.
2 Put the lobster, back upwards, on a flat surface and using a sharp knife split the lobster cleanly in two, piercing through the 'cross' at the centre of the head.
3 Remove and discard the intestine which runs through the centre of the tail, the stomach (which lies near the head) and the spongy looking gills or 'dead man's fingers', which are inedible.
4 Sprinkle the flesh with salt and pepper to taste and brush with melted butter. Cook under a medium grill for about 5 minutes.
5 Transfer to a warmed platter. Add the claws and garnish with lemon slices and parsley.

WARM SCALLOP AND BASIL SALAD

PREPARATION TIME 10 minutes
COOKING TIME 4-6 minutes
FREEZING Not suitable
◴

SERVES 6

- *50 g (2 oz) drained sun-dried tomatoes in olive oil*
- *1 small bunch fresh basil*
- *60 ml (4 tbsp) walnut oil*
- *30 ml (2 tbsp) sherry vinegar or red wine vinegar*

355 CALS/SERVING

- *selection of salad leaves, such as lollo rosso, rocket, frisée or lamb's tongue lettuce*
- *60 ml (4 tbsp) olive oil*
- *700 g (1½ lb) scallops*
- *salt and pepper*

1 Roughly chop the dried tomatoes and the basil. Whisk together the walnut oil and vinegar in a bowl. Stir in the tomatoes and basil. Place the salad leaves in a large bowl.
2 Heat the olive oil in a large sauté pan and sauté the scallops in two batches until well browned – about 2-3 minutes. Take care not to overcook.
3 Off the heat, return all the scallops to the pan. Stir in the tomato and basil mixture, adjust the seasoning and immediately pour over the salad leaves. Toss and serve on individual salad plates.

DRESSED CRAB

PREPARATION TIME 1 hour
FREEZING Not suitable
♡

SERVES 2-3

- *1 cooked crab, about 900 g (2 lb)*
- *salt and pepper*
- *15 ml (1 tbsp) lemon juice*
- *30 ml (2 tbsp) fresh white breadcrumbs*

195-130 CALS/SERVING

- *1 egg, hard-boiled*
- *15 ml (1 tbsp) chopped fresh parsley*
- *frisée lettuce, to serve*

1 Twist off the legs and claws as close to the body as possible. Break each claw in half then crack with a rolling pin or hammer without crushing the flesh. If you are not using the legs for garnishing, break the shell on the legs with your hands. Using a slender skewer to get at any awkward bits, carefully extract the flesh.
2 Put the crab on its back with the tail flap pointing towards you. Holding the shell firmly, press the body section upwards with your thumbs and it should come away. If it won't move, use the point of a rigid knife to ease it away.
3 With a teaspoon, scoop out into a separate bowl the creamy brown meat and roe (if any) from the shell. Remove and discard the stomach bag which you will find between the eyes. (If this breaks make sure you remove all the greenish or grey-white matter.)
4 Pull away from the body and discard the inedible feathery gills or 'dead man's fingers'. Using a large heavy knife, cut the body in half. Using a skewer, remove the flesh from the tiny crevices.
5 Using two forks, flake all the white meat from the crab. Season and add 5 ml (1 tsp) lemon juice.
6 Pound the brown meat in a bowl with the breadcrumbs and remaining lemon juice. Season.
7 Using a small spoon, put the white meat in both ends of the cleaned crab shell, making sure that it is well piled up in the shell. Spoon the brown meat in a neat line down the centre between the two sections of white crab meat.
8 Chop the egg white and sieve the yolk. Hold a blunt knife between the white and brown crab meat, then carefully spoon lines of parsley, egg yolk and egg white across the crab, moving the knife as you go. Serve on a bed of frisée.

MIXED SEAFOOD SALAD

PREPARATION TIME 20 minutes, plus chilling
COOKING TIME About 25 minutes
FREEZING Not suitable

SERVES 6

- *150 ml (5 fl oz) dry white wine*
- *1 bay leaf*
- *few peppercorns*
- *1 parsley sprig*
- *½ small onion, peeled and sliced*
- *350 g (12 oz) raw tiger prawns, thawed if frozen*
- *700 g (1½ lb) haddock fillet, skinned and cut into 2.5 cm (1 inch) chunks*
- *75 g (3 oz) mangetout, trimmed*
- *salt and pepper*

455 CALS/SERVING

- *450 g (1 lb) cooked mussels*
- *1 red pepper, deseeded and cut into strips*
- *2 carrots, peeled and cut into strips*
- *50 g (2 oz) pitted black olives*
- *150 ml (5 fl oz) olive oil*
- *45 ml (3 tbsp) white wine vinegar*
- *1-2 garlic cloves, peeled and crushed*
- *45 ml (3 tbsp) chopped fresh parsley*

1 Put the wine in a saucepan with 150 ml (5 fl oz) water. Add the bay leaf, peppercorns, parsley sprig and sliced onion. Bring to the boil. Add the tiger prawns and simmer for 5 minutes or until they turn pink. Lift out with a slotted spoon. Leave to cool.
2 Add the haddock to the wine mixture and simmer gently for about 5 minutes until the fish is cooked. Remove with a slotted spoon. Leave to cool.
3 Bring the wine mixture back to the boil and boil vigorously until reduced to about a quarter of its original volume. Leave to cool.
4 Cook the mangetout in boiling salted water for about 3 minutes, then drain.
5 Carefully peel the prawns. Put them in a bowl with the haddock and mussels. Add the mangetout, red pepper, carrots and olives.
6 Whisk together the oil, vinegar, garlic and chopped parsley. Strain the wine reduction and add to the dressing. Season, then pour over the salad and mix gently. Chill the salad in the refrigerator for 2 hours before serving.

STIR-FRIED CHICKEN WITH COURGETTES

PREPARATION TIME 10 minutes
COOKING TIME 7-10 minutes FREEZING Not suitable
♡ ◴

SERVES 4
- *30 ml (2 tbsp) oil*
- *1 garlic clove, peeled and crushed*
- *450 g (1 lb) skinless chicken breast fillets, sliced into strips*
- *450 g (1 lb) courgettes, sliced*

250 CALS/SERVING
- *1 red pepper, deseeded and cut into strips*
- *45 ml (3 tbsp) dry sherry*
- *15 ml (1 tbsp) light soy sauce*
- *pepper*

1 Heat the oil in a wok or a large frying pan and fry the garlic for 1 minute. Add the chicken and cook for 3-4 minutes, stirring continuously.
2 Add the courgettes and red pepper and continue to cook for 1-2 minutes, until the chicken is cooked and the vegetables are tender but still crisp.
3 Stir in the sherry and soy sauce and cook for 1 minute. Season to taste with pepper and serve.

POACHED CHICKEN IN WATERCRESS SAUCE

PREPARATION TIME 5 minutes
COOKING TIME 15 minutes
FREEZING Not suitable
♡ ◴

SERVES 4
- *4 skinless chicken breast fillets, each weighing about 125 g (4 oz)*
- *4 thin slices of Parma ham*
- *90 ml (6 tbsp) dry white wine*
- *50 ml (2 fl oz) chicken stock*

215 CALS/SERVING
- *60 ml (4 tbsp) single cream*
- *90 ml (6 tbsp) chopped watercress*
- *ground black pepper*
- *flat-leaf parsley, to garnish*

1 Wrap each chicken breast in a slice of ham. Place in a saucepan just large enough to fit the chicken in one layer.
2 Pour the wine and stock over. Bring to the boil, cover and simmer for 10-12 minutes or until the chicken is tender. Remove to a serving dish.
3 Boil down the juices to about 75 ml (5 tbsp). Add the cream and bring to the boil. Remove from the heat and mix in the watercress. Season with pepper, pour over chicken and garnish.

TIP
To serve cold, complete to the end of stage 2, then cool and thickly slice. Fold the watercress into 60 ml (4 tbsp) low-calorie mayonnaise and serve with the chicken.

LIME-PEPPERED CHICKEN

PREPARATION TIME 15 minutes, plus marinating
COOKING TIME 10-12 minutes
FREEZING Not suitable
♡

SERVES 6
- *6 skinless chicken breast fillets*
- *2 small red or yellow chillies, thinly sliced*
- *10 ml (2 tsp) coarse-ground black peppercorns*
- *shredded rind and juice of 3 limes*
- *1 garlic clove, peeled and crushed*
- *30 ml (2 tbsp) clear honey*
- *small aubergines or wedges of courgette, onion or lemon, to finish*

350 CALS/SERVING

DIPPING SAUCE
- *60 ml (4 tbsp) mango chutney*
- *1 garlic clove, peeled and crushed*
- *1 green chilli, seeded*
- *2.5 cm (1 inch) piece fresh root ginger, peeled and grated*
- *10 ml (2 tsp) light soft brown sugar*
- *10 ml (2 tsp) white wine vinegar*
- *45 ml (3 tbsp) soy sauce*
- *few drops Tabasco*
- *90 ml (6 tbsp) oil*

1 Cut the chicken into bite-size pieces. Toss together the chicken, chillies and the next four ingredients. Cover and marinate in the refrigerator for at least 10 minutes.

2 Meanwhile, make the dipping sauce. Place all the ingredients in a food processor and blend for about 15 seconds or until well combined. Cover and refrigerate until required.

3 Thread the marinated chicken pieces onto metal or wooden skewers. Thread an aubergine half, a slice of courgette or a wedge of onion or lemon on to the end of each skewer.

4 Cook on the barbecue or under a hot grill for 10-12 minutes, turning frequently, basting with the reserved marinade. Serve immediately with the sauce for dipping.

NOTE Garnish the dip with a few small mixed chillies for added colour.

It's a good idea to wear rubber gloves when preparing chillies as they can irritate the skin. Remove the seeds to reduce the hotness.

CHICKEN WITH SPICED WHEAT

PREPARATION TIME 20 minutes, plus marinating and cooling
COOKING TIME 20-24 minutes
FREEZING Not suitable
♡

SERVES 6

- *15 ml (1 tbsp) mango chutney*
- *15 ml (1 tbsp) mild curry paste*
- *10 ml (2 tsp) ground turmeric*
- *50 ml (2 fl oz) olive oil*
- *4 skinless chicken breast fillets, 575 g (1¼ lb) total weight*
- *30 ml (2 tbsp) white wine vinegar*

337 CALS/SERVING

- *175 g (6 oz) bulghur wheat*
- *salt and pepper*
- *30 ml (2 tbsp) snipped fresh chives*
- *175 g (6 oz) cherry tomatoes*
- *1 bunch spring onions, roughly chopped*
- *marjoram leaves, to garnish (optional)*

1 Mix together the chutney, curry paste and turmeric. Stir in half the oil. Cut the chicken into bite-size pieces and toss into the mixture. Cover and marinate in the refrigerator for 30 minutes, or overnight.

2 Spread the chicken pieces over a foil-lined grill pan. Cook under a hot grill in batches for 10-12 minutes until the chicken is cooked through and golden brown. Transfer to a bowl with the pan juices and stir in the remaining oil and the vinegar. Leave to cool.

3 Meanwhile, place the bulghur wheat in a bowl and pour over enough boiling water to cover. Leave to soak for about 30 minutes until all of the water has been absorbed and the grains are soft. Stir once or twice and drain well. Season to taste. Stir in the chives.

4 Drain the oil mixture from the chicken and stir into the wheat. Spoon onto a platter.

5 Halve the tomatoes. Mix together with the spring onions and chicken and spoon over the wheat. Garnish with marjoram, if wished.

MEDITERRANEAN CHICKEN

PREPARATION TIME 40 minutes
COOKING TIME About 5 minutes
FREEZING Not suitable

SERVES 6

480 CALS/SERVING

- *225 g (8 oz) courgettes*
- *olive oil*
- *10 sun-dried tomatoes in olive oil, drained, about 75 g (3 oz) total weight*
- *salt and pepper*
- *75 g (3 oz) young spinach leaves*
- *400 g (14 oz) crusty loaf*
- *350 g (12 oz) cooked skinned chicken breast fillet, thinly sliced*
- *340 g (12 oz) jar peperonata*
- *10 pitted black olives, halved*
- *300 g (10 oz) mozzarella cheese, thinly sliced*
- *10 fresh basil leaves*

1 Thinly slice the courgettes lengthways, brush lightly with olive oil and grill on each side for 3-4 minutes or until golden brown; drain and cool. Slice the sun-dried tomatoes.
2 Bring a large saucepan of salted water to the boil. Blanch the spinach leaves in batches for 10 seconds, remove with a slotted spoon and plunge into cold water. Drain well.
3 Cut away and remove the base of the loaf, leaving a border of about 2.5 cm (1 inch). Reserve the base. Hollow out the loaf so that the walls are about 1 cm (½ inch) thick. (Use the leftover bread to make breadcrumbs and freeze for use later.)
4 Drizzle the inside of the loaf with about 30 ml (2 tbsp) olive oil. Layer up the chicken, spinach, courgettes, peperonata, olives, sun-dried tomatoes, mozzarella and basil leaves, pressing well into the loaf. Season between layers.
5 When the loaf is full, replace the base. Press into shape and wrap tightly in clingfilm. Chill for at least 2 hours, preferably overnight.
6 Leave the loaf at room temperature for 1 hour before cutting into slices to serve.

NOTE Peperonata is a colourful Italian mixture of peppers, onions and tomatoes in a little oil. You'll find it with the pasta sauces in the supermarket, and in delicatessens. There's no need to drain the mixture, as the juice adds extra flavour and texture to the loaf.

CHEESY CHICKEN AND BACON ROLLS

PREPARATION TIME 10 minutes
COOKING TIME 35 minutes
FREEZING Suitable (stage 2)
❄

SERVES 4

600 CALS/SERVING (WITHOUT DIP)

- *12 boneless, skinless chicken thighs, about 700 g (1½ lb) total weight*
- *30 ml (2 tbsp) wholegrain mustard*
- *125 g (4 oz) Gruyère cheese*
- *12 slices lightly smoked streaky bacon, about 250 g (9 oz)*
- *Garlic Dip, to serve (see Tip)*

1 Unroll each chicken thigh and spread the inside with mustard. Cut the cheese into 12 fat sticks and place on top of the mustard. Roll up the chicken.
2 Gently stretch the bacon with the back of a knife and wrap one piece tightly around each thigh. Secure with wooden satay sticks.
3 Place the chicken rolls in a non-stick roasting tin and bake at 190°C (375°F) mark 5 for 30-35 minutes or until cooked through and golden brown. Serve immediately with Garlic Dip.

VARIATION Other types of cheese can be used inside these chicken pieces. Try Cheddar or Emmental.

TIP

For an instant Garlic Dip just beat equal quantities of fromage frais and mayonnaise with a little crushed garlic. Top with crispy grilled bacon and black pepper.

GRILLED CHICKEN SALAD

PREPARATION TIME 15 minutes, plus cooling
COOKING TIME 30 minutes
FREEZING Not suitable
♡

SERVES 4

350 CALS/SERVING

- *175 g (6 oz) ripe tomatoes, halved*
- *30 ml (2 tbsp) tapenade (black olive paste)*
- *olive oil*
- *4 skinless chicken breast fillets, each weighing about 125 g (4 oz)*

DRESSING

- *1 shallot, peeled and finely chopped*
- *45 ml (3 tbsp) olive oil*
- *15 ml (1 tbsp) walnut oil*
- *20 ml (4 tsp) white wine vinegar*
- *30 ml (2 tbsp) single cream*
- *15 ml (1 tbsp) chopped fresh basil*
- *salt and pepper*
- *mixed salad, to serve, such as green leaves, cherry tomatoes, olives, onions and cooked globe artichoke hearts*

1 Grill the tomatoes skin-side up until black and charred. Purée in a blender or food processor with the olive paste and a little olive oil, if necessary, to give a thinnish paste.
2 Place the chicken skinned-side down on a foil-lined grill pan. Brush lightly with olive oil and grill for 7-8 minutes.
3 Turn the chicken skinned-side up and grill for 5 minutes. Spoon the tomato paste over the chicken and grill for a further 5-6 minutes or until the chicken is cooked through and the topping is well browned. Cool, cover, then refrigerate for at least 1 hour to firm up.
4 Meanwhile, make the dressing. Whisk the shallot with the olive oil, walnut oil, vinegar, cream, basil and salt and pepper to taste. Set aside.
5 Thickly slice the chicken and serve with a selection of salad ingredients. Spoon over the dressing.

SMOKED CHICKEN WITH CUCUMBER AND MANGO

PREPARATION TIME 45 minutes, plus chilling
FREEZING Not suitable

SERVES 6

370 CALS/SERVING

- *1.1 kg (2½ lb) smoked chicken*
- *1 small cucumber*
- *1 large, ripe mango*
- *grated rind and juice of 2 limes*
- *150 ml (5 fl oz) vegetable oil*
- *30 ml (2 tbsp) chopped fresh coriander*
- *1 bunch spring onions, trimmed and finely chopped*
- *salt and pepper*

1 Slice the chicken flesh into 5 cm (2 inch) pieces, discarding skin and bone. You should end up with about 700 g (1½ lb) chicken flesh.
2 Halve the cucumber lengthways and remove the seeds with a teaspoon. Slice on the diagonal, then leave to drain on absorbent kitchen paper for about 30 minutes.
3 Cut down either side of the mango stone. Cut away the flesh from the skin and place in a blender or food processor, with the grated lime rind and strained lime juice. Process until smooth. Keep the processor running and add the oil in a slow, steady stream.
4 Pour the mango dressing into a large bowl and mix in all the remaining ingredients, adding seasoning to taste. Cover and chill for up to a day before serving.

NOTE Smoked chicken is available from larger supermarkets. Alternatively, use 350 g (12 oz) smoked ham and 350 g (12 oz) cooked chicken.

WARM DUCK SALAD

PREPARATION TIME 20 minutes
COOKING TIME 15-20 minutes
FREEZING Not suitable
♡

SERVES 8

- *8 boned duckling breasts, each weighing about 125 g (4 oz)*
- *30 ml (2 tbsp) ground coriander*
- *10 ml (2 tsp) ground ginger*
- *10 ml (2 tsp) ground mace*
- *1 garlic clove, peeled and crushed*
- *75 ml (3 fl oz) fresh orange juice*

325 CALS/SERVING

- *75 ml (3 fl oz) olive oil*
- *salt and pepper*
- *7.5 ml (1½ tsp) clear honey*
- *15 ml (1 tbsp) red wine vinegar*
- *7.5 ml (1½ tsp) Dijon mustard*
- *selection of mixed salad leaves, to line the dish*
- *about 20 pitted black olives*

1 Remove the skin from the duck. Mix together the coriander, ginger, mace and garlic with 30 ml (2 tbsp) each of orange juice and oil. Season with salt and pepper.

2 Spread the spice mixture on both sides of the duck breasts and place in a shallow ovenproof dish. Roast at 200°C (400°F) mark 6 for 15-20 minutes until the duckling is tender and the top has browned.

3 Meanwhile, whisk together the honey, vinegar, mustard and remaining orange juice and oil. Season to taste. Wash the salad leaves, dry them and arrange on a shallow platter.

4 Lift the duck breasts out of the pan juices, slice neatly and arrange on the salad leaves. Scatter the olives over the top and spoon over the dressing.

VARIATION If wished, the duck can be cooked in advance and served cold.

MIDDLE EASTERN MEAT SKEWERS

PREPARATION TIME 25 minutes
COOKING TIME 15 minutes
FREEZING Suitable (stage 2)
❄

SERVES 6
- *900 g (2 lb) minced beef or lamb*
- *2 onions, peeled and grated*
- *30 ml (2 tbsp) ground cumin*
- *15 ml (1 tbsp) coarsely ground coriander*
- *90 ml (6 tbsp) finely chopped fresh parsley*
- *salt and pepper*

415 CALS/SERVING
- *olive oil*
- *paprika*
- *lemon wedges, to serve*

MINTED YOGURT SAUCE
- *3 spring onions*
- *300 ml (10 fl oz) natural yogurt*
- *15 ml (1 tbsp) chopped fresh mint*

1 Get your butcher to mince the meat three times, or chop it in a food processor until very fine. Knead it with the grated onion, cumin, coriander, 60 ml (4 tbsp) parsley and seasoning to make a smooth paste.
2 Take about 15-30 ml (1-2 tbsp) of the mixture and press a flat sausage shape onto the ends of wooden skewers. Brush them lightly with oil and sprinkle with a little paprika.
3 Grill about half the kebabs at a time under a high heat for about 5 minutes. Turn, sprinkle with more paprika and grill the second side until well browned all over. (Keep the exposed wooden sticks away from the heat.)
4 Keep the kebabs warm, loosely covered, until they are all cooked. Sprinkle with parsley.
5 Meanwhile, make the sauce. Chop the spring onions, reserving a few dark green shreds for garnish, and mix with the yogurt and mint. Serve with the kebabs and lemon wedges.

SESAME BEEF SALAD

PREPARATION TIME 20 minutes, plus marinating
COOKING TIME 15 minutes
FREEZING Not suitable
♡

SERVES 6

215 CALS/SERVING

- *30 ml (2 tbsp) soy sauce*
- *30 ml (2 tbsp) Worcestershire sauce*
- *30 ml (2 tbsp) soft brown sugar*
- *10 ml (2 tsp) tomato purée*
- *5 ml (1 tsp) lemon juice*
- *15 ml (1 tbsp) white wine vinegar*
- *20 ml (4 tsp) sesame seeds*
- *vegetable oil*
- *2 garlic cloves, peeled and crushed*
- *salt and pepper*
- *700 g (1½ lb) rump steak*
- *6 sticks celery*
- *1 bunch spring onions*
- *1 small cucumber*

1 Mix the first seven ingredients together in a bowl with 30 ml (2 tbsp) oil, the garlic and seasoning. Slice the steak into strips 5 mm (¼ inch) thick and 5 cm (2 inches) long. Stir the strips into the marinade. Cover and leave to marinate in the refrigerator for at least 3 hours, until ready to cook.
2 Cut the celery, spring onions and cucumber (discarding the seeds) into thin matchsticks. Refrigerate in a polythene bag until ready to use.
3 Heat a little oil in a large wok or non-stick frying pan until the oil begins to smoke. Lift the steak strips from the marinade and fry in small batches until they are well browned. Place them in a large bowl.
4 Add the rest of the marinade to the pan and reduce until it forms a syrup. Pour over the steak strips. Either stir all the vegetables in with the steak or serve separately.

TIP
This makes an excellent quick after-work meal as all the ingredients can be prepared at least 24 hours in advance and cooked at the last minute just before serving.

PIZZAIOLA STEAK

PREPARATION TIME 15 minutes
COOKING TIME 10 minutes
FREEZING Not suitable
♡ ◴

SERVES 4

340 CALS/SERVING

- *60 ml (4 tbsp) olive oil*
- *4 thin rump steaks*
- *2 garlic cloves, peeled and crushed*
- *salt and pepper*
- *450 g (1 lb) firm red tomatoes, skinned and chopped*
- *45 ml (3 tbsp) chopped fresh basil*
- *15 ml (1 tbsp) chopped fresh parsley*
- *basil sprigs, to garnish*

1 Heat the oil in a large frying pan, add the steaks and fry quickly over a high heat for 2-3 minutes until browned on both sides. Add the garlic and salt and pepper to taste and fry for 30 seconds.
2 Add the tomatoes and herbs and cook for 3-5 minutes until the tomatoes are softened and the juices reduced. Adjust the seasoning and serve at once, garnished with basil sprigs.

TOMATO-CRUSTED LAMB WITH SUMMER VEGETABLES

PREPARATION TIME 20 minutes
COOKING TIME About 1 hour
FREEZING Not suitable

SERVES 6

550 CALS/SERVING

- *2 garlic cloves, peeled*
- *100 ml (4 fl oz) olive oil*
- *125 g (4 oz) sun-dried tomatoes*
- *5 ml (1 tsp) chopped fresh thyme or 2.5 ml (½ tsp) dried thyme*
- *salt and pepper*
- *2 racks of lamb (about 7 cutlets each), chined*
- *450 g (1 lb) new potatoes, roughly chopped*
- *450 g (1 lb) young carrots, peeled and roughly chopped*
- *450 g (1 lb) summer squash, peeled and roughly chopped*
- *about 18 pitted black olives*
- *1.25 ml (¼ tsp) fennel seeds*
- *juice of 1 lemon*
- *5 ml (1 tsp) caster sugar*
- *chopped flat-leaf parsley, to garnish*

1 In a blender or food processor, blend together the garlic, 30 ml (2 tbsp) of the olive oil, the tomatoes and thyme to a smooth paste. Season with salt and pepper. Trim the lamb of most of the fat and score at regular intervals. Press the tomato mixture firmly over the lamb to coat.
2 Blanch the potatoes in boiling, salted water for 1-2 minutes, then drain. Toss the potatoes, carrots and squash in a roasting tin with the olives, fennel seeds, lemon juice, sugar and remaining oil.
3 Roast the vegetables, uncovered, at 220°C (425°F) mark 7 for about 30 minutes or until just tender. Place the lamb on a rack over the vegetables and cook for about 25 minutes for medium rare, or about 30-35 minutes for well done. Cover the lamb loosely with foil if the crust starts to burn.
4 Remove the lamb from the oven and leave to rest in a warm place for 5 minutes before carving. Transfer the vegetables to a serving dish.
5 Carve the lamb into cutlets and serve with the vegetables. Pour any pan juices over the lamb. Garnish with chopped flat-leaf parsley.

MINTED LAMB ESCALOPES

PREPARATION TIME 10 minutes, plus marinating
COOKING TIME 6 minutes
FREEZING Not suitable
♡

SERVES 4

210 CALS/SERVING

- *90 ml (6 tbsp) Greek natural yogurt*
- *1 garlic clove, peeled and crushed*
- *60 ml (4 tbsp) chopped fresh mint*
- *30 ml (2 tbsp) lemon juice*
- *450 g (1 lb) lamb escalopes*
- *salt and pepper*
- *mint leaves, to garnish*
- *warm pitta bread and tomato and onion salad, to serve*

1 Mix the yogurt, garlic, chopped mint, and lemon juice with the lamb. Season with salt and pepper. Place in a non-metallic dish, cover and marinate in the refrigerator for 2-3 hours.
2 Spread the lamb in a grill pan and grill for 3 minutes on each side or until golden brown.
3 Garnish with mint and serve immediately with some warm pitta bread and tomato and onion salad.

NOTE For this recipe, you need very thin lean escalopes cut from the leg. These are sold ready-prepared in some supermarkets; alternatively ask your butcher to prepare them for you.

VARIATION For spiced lamb escalopes, replace the mint with 5 ml (1 tsp) each ground cumin and turmeric, and 2.5 cm (1 inch) piece fresh root ginger, grated.

PEPPERED GARLIC PORK WITH CREME FRAICHE

PREPARATION TIME 30 minutes
COOKING TIME 40-45 minutes
FREEZING Not suitable
♡

SERVES 6

- *2 pork tenderloins, each weighing about 350 g (12 oz)*
- *salt*
- *60 ml (4 tbsp) olive oil*
- *8 shallots, peeled and chopped*
- *6 garlic cloves, peeled and chopped*
- *15 ml (1 tbsp) coarsely crushed green peppercorns*
- *30 ml (2 tbsp) mixed chopped fresh chives and parsley*

350 CALS/SERVING

- *25 g (1 oz) fresh white breadcrumbs*
- *30 ml (2 tbsp) beaten egg*
- *450 ml (15 fl oz) chicken stock*
- *150 ml (5 fl oz) medium dry white wine*
- *60 ml (4 tbsp) crème fraîche*

1 Trim the pork tenderloins and cut a lengthways slit about halfway into each one, then open out flat. Cover with a piece of clingfilm and beat with a meat mallet or rolling pin until the pork is a rectangular shape about 1 cm (½ inch) thick. Season with salt.
2 Heat half the oil in a saucepan, add the shallots and garlic and fry gently for 5 minutes. Remove from the heat and add the peppercorns, herbs and breadcrumbs. Mix well, then stir in the egg.
3 Press the mixture along the middle of each tenderloin. Close the pork and tie at regular intervals with fine string.
4 Heat the remaining oil in a frying pan, add the tenderloins, cutting in half if necessary to fit into the frying pan, and brown all over. Transfer to a roasting tin and drizzle with any juices in pan. Add 200 ml (7 fl oz) stock to the roasting tin.
5 Cook in the oven at 190°C (375°F) mark 5 for 30-35 minutes or until cooked through, basting frequently with the juices. Remove the pork tenderloins to a serving plate and keep warm.
6 Add the remaining stock and the wine to the roasting pan and boil rapidly until reduced by one-third. Add the crème fraîche and boil for 3 minutes until smooth and creamy.
7 Remove the string from the pork and cut the pork into neat slices. Serve hot with the sauce.

VARIATION For a richer flavour, add 75 g (3 oz) sliced mushrooms with the crème fraîche at stage 6 and boil for 3 minutes, stirring occasionally.

MAPLE-GLAZED GAMMON WITH PAPAYA SALSA

PREPARATION TIME 20 minutes, plus cooling
COOKING TIME 2½ hours
FREEZING Not suitable

SERVES 10-12

- *2.3 kg (5 lb) piece smoked gammon*
- *1 bay leaf*
- *few parsley stalks*
- *30 ml (2 tbsp) maple syrup*
- *10 ml (2 tsp) American mustard*
- *40 g (1½ oz) soft brown sugar*

PAPAYA SALSA

- *1 ripe papaya*
- *3-4 spring onions, trimmed and finely chopped*
- *1 fresh green chilli, deseeded and finely chopped*
- *30-45 ml (2-3 tbsp) chopped fresh coriander*
- *juice of 1 lime*
- *salt*

415-350 CALS/SERVING

1 Place the gammon in a large saucepan, cover with cold water and add the bay leaf and parsley stalks. Bring slowly to the boil, reduce the heat, cover and simmer gently for 2 hours.

2 Remove the gammon from the pan, allow to cool slightly, then strip off the skin, leaving the layer of fat on the joint.

3 Place the gammon joint in a roasting tin. Score the fat into a diamond pattern, cutting through the layer of fat each time, but taking care not to cut into the flesh. Mix the maple syrup with the mustard and sugar and spread over the scored fat.

4 Cook in the oven at 190°C (375°F) mark 5 for 20-30 minutes until the fat is glazed and golden brown; baste frequently with the juices in tin. Remove from the oven and leave to cool.

5 About 30 minutes before serving, prepare the papaya salsa. Halve the papaya and scoop out the seeds. Remove the peel and dice the flesh. Place in a serving bowl. Add the remaining ingredients, seasoning with salt to taste, and mix well.

6 Carve the gammon into slices and serve with the papaya salsa.

VARIATION The boiled and glazed gammon joint is also extremely good served hot with seasonal vegetables, such as baby broad beans, peas or green beans and buttered new potatoes.

HOMEMADE SAUSAGES WITH ROCKET PESTO

PREPARATION TIME 20 minutes, plus chilling
COOKING TIME 10-12 minutes
FREEZING Suitable (stage 2)
❄

SERVES 6

- *125 g (4 oz) rindless smoked streaky bacon, finely chopped*
- *450 g (1 lb) lean minced pork*
- *225 g (8 oz) pork sausagemeat*
- *1 small red chilli, deseeded and finely chopped*
- *2 garlic cloves, peeled and crushed*
- *25 g (1 oz) fresh white breadcrumbs*
- *salt and pepper*
- *1 egg plus 1 egg yolk*

495 CALS/SERVING

ROCKET PESTO

- *75 g (3 oz) goats' cheese or low-fat soft cheese*
- *25 g (1 oz) Gruyère or Emmental cheese, grated*
- *200 ml (7 fl oz) olive oil*
- *25 g (1 oz) shelled pistachio nuts*
- *1 garlic clove, peeled*
- *2.5 ml (½ tsp) salt*
- *75 g (3 oz) rocket leaves or watercress*

1 Mix together the bacon, minced pork, sausagemeat, chilli, garlic and breadcrumbs. Season with salt and pepper, then beat in the egg and egg yolk.
2 Shape the mixture into about 18 sausages. Cover and chill for at least 15 minutes and preferably overnight.
3 Cook the sausages on the barbecue for about 10-12 minutes or until cooked through.
4 To make the rocket pesto, blend all the ingredients in a blender or food processor until smooth.
5 Serve the sausages with the rocket pesto as a dip.

VARIATION To oven-cook the sausages, heat 60 ml (4 tbsp) olive oil in a large roasting tin on the hob. Add the sausages in batches and brown on all sides. Return the sausages to the tin and cook in the oven at 200°C (400°F) mark 6 for 20-25 minutes or until cooked through.

CHINESE-STYLE SPARE RIBS

PREPARATION TIME 5 minutes
COOKING TIME 60-70 minutes
FREEZING Not suitable
♡

SERVES 4-6

- *900 g (2 lb) lean pork ribs*
- *30 ml (2 tbsp) vegetable oil*
- *salt*
- *spring onion and orange rind strips, to garnish*

SAUCE

- *2.5 cm (1 inch) piece fresh root ginger, peeled and finely chopped*

295-195 CALS/SERVING

- *1 garlic clove, peeled and chopped*
- *60 ml (4 tbsp) clear honey*
- *30 ml (2 tbsp) dark soy sauce*
- *30 ml (2 tbsp) tomato ketchup*
- *2 good pinches of five-spice powder*
- *150 ml (5 fl oz) unsweetened orange juice*

1 Cut the ribs into smaller pieces, if wished. Heat the oil in a large frying pan, add the ribs and season well with salt. Fry the ribs over a moderate heat for about 10 minutes, turning frequently.
2 Mix together all the sauce ingredients and pour over the ribs. Cover the pan and cook gently for 50-60 minutes or until the meat is tender and the sauce is reduced to a sticky syrup, turning the ribs occasionally.
3 Arrange the ribs on a hot serving plate and garnish with spring onion and orange rind strips.

COURGETTE AND BACON FRITTATA

PREPARATION TIME 10 minutes
COOKING TIME 6-10 minutes
FREEZING Not suitable
♡ ◴

SERVES 4 — 160 CALS/SERVING

- *15 ml (1 tbsp) vegetable oil*
- *450 g (1 lb) courgettes, thickly sliced*
- *125 g (4 oz) rindless smoked streaky bacon, chopped*
- *50 g (2 oz) onion, peeled and chopped*
- *30 ml (2 tbsp) chopped fresh thyme*
- *15 ml (1 tbsp) chopped fresh rosemary*
- *2 eggs*
- *salt and pepper*
- *chopped fresh herbs, to garnish*

1 Heat the oil in a non-stick 20-25 cm (8-10 inch) frying pan. Sauté the courgettes, bacon and onion together for 4-5 minutes, stirring continuously, until just beginning to soften and turn golden brown.
2 Whisk together the thyme, rosemary and eggs. Season with salt and pepper. Pour over the courgette mixture and leave to set over a low heat for 2-3 minutes. Serve immediately, cut into wedges and sprinkled with chopped fresh herbs.

VEGETABLE EGG NESTS

PREPARATION TIME 15 minutes
COOKING TIME 15 minutes
FREEZING Not suitable
♡ ◴

SERVES 4 — 240 CALS/SERVING

- *450 g (1 lb) trimmed leeks, sliced*
- *550 g (1¼ lb) courgettes, sliced*
- *225 g (8 oz) asparagus tips*
- *125 g (4 oz) peas*
- *50 g (2 oz) low-fat spread*
- *30 ml (2 tbsp) chopped fresh parsley*
- *1 garlic clove, peeled and crushed*
- *salt and pepper*
- *4 eggs*
- *8 anchovy fillets*

1 Steam the leeks, courgettes and asparagus for about 12-15 minutes or until tender, adding the peas for the last 5 minutes of cooking time.
2 Meanwhile, mix together the low-fat spread, parsley and garlic. Season well.
3 Poach the eggs in gently simmering water for 4-5 minutes or until just set.
4 Divide the hot vegetables among four individual dishes. Make a well in the centre and place an egg in each. Season each egg with pepper and cross two anchovy fillets on top. Top the vegetables with a little herb mixture to serve.

NOTE Many people believe that brown eggs are more nutritious than white, but this is not the case – the only difference is the colour of the shell.

VARIATION Vary the vegetables according to what is available – steamed baby sweetcorn, baby carrots and small broccoli florets will also work well in this dish.

FETA AND OREGANO TARTS

PREPARATION TIME 20 minutes, plus chilling
COOKING TIME 45 minutes
FREEZING Suitable (stage 1)
❄

MAKES 6

435 CALS/TART

- *Shortcrust Pastry, made with 225 g (8 oz) white plain flour (see page 75)*
- *300 g (10 oz) tomatoes, skinned*
- *175 g (6 oz) feta cheese, roughly chopped*
- *45 ml (3 tbsp) chopped fresh oregano*
- *2 eggs, beaten*
- *150 ml (5 fl oz) single cream*
- *pepper*

1 Roll out the pastry and use to line six 9 cm (3½ inch) flan tins about 2.5 cm (1 inch) deep. Chill for about 30 minutes then bake the pastry blind (see page 75) for 20 minutes or until golden.
2 Cut each tomato into 6-8 pieces, discarding the seeds. Place the feta cheese in a bowl. Stir in the oregano, eggs and cream.
3 Fill each tart case with a little of the mixture to come to within 5 mm (¼ inch) of the top of the pastry. Arrange the tomato pieces over the top of each flan.
4 Bake at 180°C (350°F) mark 4 for about 25 minutes or until just set and beginning to brown. Cool for 10 minutes. Grind over pepper and serve.

NOTE These tarts can be made a day in advance. Store them in the refrigerator and serve at room temperature.

TIP

These individual tarts are ideal for picnics. Allow to cool completely and wrap each one in foil before packing in a rigid container.

ITALIAN SEAFOOD PASTA SALAD

PREPARATION TIME 15 minutes, plus marinating
COOKING TIME 15-20 minutes
FREEZING Not suitable

SERVES 6

- *225 g (8 oz) dried pasta twists*
- *1 small red pepper, quartered and deseeded*
- *two 225 g (8 oz) packets cooked mixed seafood*
- *6 each black and green olives, pitted and quartered*
- *flat-leaf parsley sprigs, to garnish*

440 CALS/SERVING

DRESSING

- *60 ml (4 tbsp) balsamic or white wine vinegar*
- *150 ml (5 fl oz) olive oil*
- *2 garlic cloves, peeled and crushed*
- *45 ml (3 tbsp) chopped fresh parsley*
- *salt and pepper*

1 Bring a large pan of salted water to the boil, add the pasta and cook for 10-12 minutes until just tender (*al dente*). Drain, rinse in cold water and drain again, then leave to cool.
2 Meanwhile, grill the pepper, skin-side up, for 5-8 minutes until the skin is blistering and beginning to blacken. Place the pepper quarters in a polythene bag, seal tightly and leave to cool.
3 Place the mixed seafood in a large bowl, add the olives and set aside.
4 To make the dressing, whisk together the vinegar, olive oil, garlic and parsley and season with salt and pepper. Pour over the seafood mixture and leave to marinate at room temperature for 20 minutes.
5 When the pepper is cool, peel off the skin, rinse the pepper under cold water and pat dry with absorbent kitchen paper. Shred finely and add to the seafood with the pasta. Toss lightly to mix, garnish with flat-leaf parsley sprigs and serve.

PASTA WITH WALNUT AND BASIL SAUCE

PREPARATION TIME 15 minutes
COOKING TIME 12 minutes
FREEZING Not suitable

SERVES 4

- *2 large garlic cloves, peeled*
- *40 g (1½ oz) fresh basil leaves (a large bunch)*
- *50 g (2 oz) freshly grated Parmesan cheese*
- *1 small tomato, skinned and deseeded*
- *60 ml (4 tbsp) olive oil*
- *salt and pepper*

480 CALS/SERVING

- *350 g (12 oz) fresh pasta or 225 g (8 oz) dried*
- *45 ml (3 tbsp) single cream*
- *50 g (2 oz) walnut pieces, chopped*
- *basil sprigs*
- *freshly grated Parmesan, to serve*

1 Place the garlic, basil leaves, Parmesan cheese and tomato flesh in a blender or food processor and work to a smooth paste.
2 Gradually add the olive oil, drop by drop, as if making mayonnaise. Season the mixture with salt and pepper to taste.
3 Cook the pasta in plenty of boiling, salted water until it is just tender (*al dente*). Drain well. Toss in a warmed serving bowl with the cream, basil sauce and walnuts. Serve immediately with fresh basil sprigs and freshly grated Parmesan cheese.

THAI CHICKEN NOODLE SALAD

PREPARATION TIME 20 minutes, plus marinating
COOKING TIME 20 minutes
FREEZING Not suitable

SERVES 6

415 CALS/SERVING

- *450 g (1 lb) skinless chicken breast fillets, cut into thick strips*
- *5 ml (1 tsp) caster sugar*
- *2.5 ml (½ tsp) salt*
- *2.5 ml (½ tsp) pepper*
- *2.5 ml (½ tsp) ground ginger*
- *2.5 ml (½ tsp) English mustard powder*
- *2.5 ml (½ tsp) ground turmeric*
- *2.5 ml (½ tsp) medium curry powder*
- *60 ml (4 tbsp) olive oil*
- *350 g (12 oz) courgettes, sliced*
- *150 g (5 oz) mangetout, trimmed*
- *1 each red and yellow pepper, deseeded and cut into strips*
- *45 ml (3 tbsp) clear honey*
- *60 ml (4 tbsp) lemon juice*
- *2.5 cm (1 inch) piece fresh root ginger, peeled and chopped*
- *250 g (9 oz) medium egg noodles*
- *50 g (2 oz) salted cashew nuts*

1 Mix the chicken with the sugar and all the seasonings. Cover and chill overnight.
2 Heat half the oil in a frying pan, add the courgettes and sauté for 2-3 minutes. Remove with a slotted spoon and transfer to a large bowl. Add the mangetout and peppers to the pan and sauté for 2-3 minutes. Add to the courgettes.
3 Heat the remaining oil and sauté the chicken in batches until golden brown. Return all the chicken to the pan and stir in the honey, lemon juice and ginger. Cover and simmer for about 5 minutes or until the chicken is quite tender.
4 Meanwhile, cook the noodles according to the packet instructions. Drain and snip into smaller pieces. Mix with the chicken and vegetables. Season with salt and pepper to taste. Sprinkle with the nuts and serve warm or cold.

PASTA IN SWEET PEPPER SAUCE

PREPARATION TIME 10 minutes
COOKING TIME 45 minutes
FREEZING Suitable (stage 2 – before adding salami)
❄

SERVES 4

360 CALS/SERVING

- *15 ml (1 tbsp) oil*
- *450 g (1 lb) red peppers, deseeded and finely chopped*
- *225 g (8 oz) onion, peeled and finely chopped*
- *1 garlic clove, peeled and crushed*
- *400 g (14 oz) can chopped tomatoes*
- *600 ml (1 pint) stock*
- *salt and pepper*
- *225 g (8 oz) dried pasta*
- *50 g (2 oz) salami, roughly chopped*
- *25 g (1 oz) freshly grated Parmesan cheese*
- *60 ml (4 tbsp) chopped fresh basil, to garnish*

1 Heat the oil and sauté the peppers, onion and garlic for 5-7 minutes or until they begin to soften.
2 Stir in the tomatoes and stock. Cover and simmer gently for 25-30 minutes or until the peppers are soft. Uncover and boil until most of the liquid has evaporated. Adjust the seasoning and add the salami.
3 Meanwhile, cook the pasta in boiling, salted water until just tender (*al dente*). Drain. Serve with the sauce, sprinkled with Parmesan cheese and garnished with fresh basil.

CRUNCHY COURGETTE PASTA

PREPARATION TIME 15 minutes
COOKING TIME 15 minutes
FREEZING Not suitable

SERVES 4

260 CALS/SERVING

- *175 g (6 oz) dried pasta*
- *salt and pepper*
- *15 ml (1 tbsp) vegetable oil*
- *125 g (4 oz) onion, peeled and finely chopped*
- *1 garlic clove, peeled and crushed*
- *1.25 ml (1/4 tsp) mild chilli powder*
- *1 red pepper, halved and chopped*
- *225 g (8 oz) tomatoes, diced*
- *225 g (8 oz) courgettes, diced*
- *350 ml (12 fl oz) tomato juice*
- *15 ml (1 tbsp) red wine vinegar*
- *30 ml (2 tbsp) chopped fresh parsley*
- *20 ml (4 tsp) freshly grated Parmesan cheese*

1 Cook the pasta in boiling, salted water until just tender (*al dente*), then drain.
2 Meanwhile, heat the oil in a non-stick frying pan and cook the onion and garlic for about 3 minutes or until beginning to soften. Stir in the chilli powder and cook for a further minute.
3 Add the red pepper, tomatoes and courgettes to the frying pan and cook over a medium heat for about 5 minutes or until hot but still crunchy. Stir in the tomato juice and vinegar with plenty of seasoning. Bring to the boil and simmer for 2-3 minutes or until piping hot.
4 Spoon the sauce over the cooked pasta and serve immediately, sprinkled with the chopped parsley and Parmesan cheese.

TOMATO AND MOZZARELLA NOODLES

PREPARATION TIME 10 minutes
COOKING TIME 10 minutes
FREEZING Not suitable

SERVES 4

410 CALS/SERVING

- *225 g (8 oz) mozzarella cheese*
- *450 g (1 lb) tomatoes, deseeded and roughly chopped*
- *grated rind of 1 lemon*
- *45 ml (3 tbsp) balsamic vinegar*
- *salt and pepper*
- *225 g (8 oz) dried pasta noodles, such as pappardelle*
- *15 ml (1 tbsp) olive oil*
- *15 ml (1 tbsp) chopped fresh thyme*

1 Dice the mozzarella cheese and set aside. Place the tomatoes in a saucepan with the lemon rind and balsamic vinegar and season with salt and pepper.
2 Meanwhile, cook the pasta in boiling, salted water until just tender (*al dente*). Drain well. Toss in the olive oil with the fresh thyme.
3 Warm the tomato mixture for 2-3 minutes and spoon it over the pasta. Top with mozzarella cheese and serve immediately.

VARIATION Try cubes of dolcelatta cheese instead of the mozzarella.

If you like garlic, sauté 2 crushed garlic cloves in a little olive oil and add to the tomato mixture at stage 3.

PASTA WITH GRILLED ASPARAGUS AND BROAD BEANS

PREPARATION TIME 20 minutes
COOKING TIME 12-15 minutes
FREEZING Not suitable

SERVES 4

- *225 g (8 oz) shelled broad beans*
- *salt and pepper*
- *350 g (12 oz) dried pasta*
- *450 g (1 lb) asparagus, trimmed and halved crossways*
- *90 ml (6 tbsp) extra-virgin olive oil*
- *2 garlic cloves, peeled and crushed*

665 CALS/SERVING

- *grated rind and juice of 1 lemon*
- *45 ml (3 tbsp) chopped fresh mint*
- *60 ml (4 tbsp) single cream*
- *60 ml (4 tbsp) grated Pecorino or Parmesan cheese*

1 Blanch the beans in a large saucepan of lightly salted water for 2 minutes, then strain the water into a clean pan and reserve. Refresh the beans under cold running water and carefully remove the hard outer skin. Reserve the beans.
2 Return the bean water to a rolling boil, add the pasta, return to the boil and cook for 10 minutes until just tender (*al dente*).
3 Meanwhile, place the asparagus on the grill pan, brush with a little oil and grill for 3-4 minutes on each side until charred and tender.
4 While the asparagus is cooking, heat 30 ml (2 tbsp) of the oil in a pan, add the garlic and lemon rind and fry gently for 3 minutes until almost golden. Add the beans, mint and cream and heat gently.
5 Drain the pasta and immediately toss with the remaining oil, transfer to a warmed bowl and stir in the asparagus and the bean sauce. Stir in the cheese and lemon juice, then season to taste. Serve at once.

VARIATION Fresh peas also combine well with asparagus and mint and can be used instead of the broad beans if wished.

STUFFED PEPPERS WITH PINE NUTS

PREPARATION TIME 20 minutes
COOKING TIME 30-35 minutes
FREEZING Not suitable
♡

SERVES 4

315 CALS SERVING

- *2 large orange or red peppers*
- *2 large yellow peppers*

FILLING

- *45 ml (3 tbsp) extra-virgin olive oil*
- *1 large onion, peeled and finely chopped*
- *2-3 garlic cloves, peeled and finely chopped*
- *450 g (1 lb) tomatoes, skinned and roughly chopped*
- *30 ml (2 tbsp) tomato purée*
- *5 ml (1 tsp) light muscovado sugar*
- *salt and pepper*
- *50 g (2 oz) mushrooms, thickly sliced*
- *50 g (2 oz) pine nuts*
- *15 ml (1 tbsp) fresh marjoram leaves, roughly torn*
- *50 g (2 oz) black olives*
- *25-50 g (1-2 oz) freshly grated Parmesan cheese*

1 Halve the peppers lengthways, then remove the core and seeds. Place cut-side down on a baking sheet and roast at 200°C (400°F) mark 6 for 15 minutes, turning frequently.
2 Meanwhile, make the sauce. Heat 30 ml (2 tbsp) oil in a saucepan, add the onion and garlic and fry gently until softened and lightly coloured. Add the tomatoes, tomato purée, sugar, salt and pepper. Cook, uncovered, for 15-20 minutes until reduced to a thick sauce. Check the seasoning.
3 Heat the remaining 15 ml (1 tbsp) oil in a pan and sauté the mushroom slices until softened.
4 Place the peppers, cut-side up, in an ovenproof dish. Transfer two thirds of the tomato mixture to a bowl and stir in the mushrooms, nuts, marjoram and olives. Fill the peppers with the mixture and top with the grated Parmesan cheese. Bake in the oven for 15-20 minutes until thoroughly heated through.

NOTE Use any remaining sauce to make a tasty accompaniment. Spread thick slices of crusty bread with the tomato mixture and sprinkle with sesame seeds. Warm through in the oven.

VEGETABLE PITHIVIER

PREPARATION TIME 1 hour, plus cooling
COOKING TIME About 1½ hours
FREEZING Not suitable

SERVES 6

585 CALS/SERVING

- *4 red peppers*
- *50 g (2 oz) butter*
- *125 g (4 oz) shallots, peeled and finely diced*
- *125 g (4 oz) mushrooms, sliced*
- *75 ml (3 fl oz) double cream or crème fraîche*
- *15 ml (1 tbsp) Parmesan cheese*
- *225 g (8 oz) ricotta cheese*
- *salt and pepper*
- *125 g (4 oz) goats' cheese*
- *450 g (1 lb) fresh spinach, washed*
- *freshly grated nutmeg*
- *450 g (1 lb) Puff Pastry (see page 75)*
- *1 egg, beaten*

1 Roast the peppers in the oven at 200°C (400°F) mark 6 for 30-40 minutes. Remove their skins and slice the flesh into strips.
2 Meanwhile, melt 40 g (1½ oz) of the butter in a frying pan, add the shallots and sauté until soft. Add the mushrooms to the pan and cook until the liquid has evaporated. Pour in the cream and allow to bubble until the mushrooms are just coated in the cream. Cool. Stir in the Parmesan and half the ricotta. Add salt and pepper.
3 Crumble the rest of the ricotta and the goats' cheese. Set aside.
4 Melt the remaining butter in a large saucepan. Add the spinach and sauté until the leaves wilt. Drain and press out any excess moisture; roughly chop. Season with salt, pepper and nutmeg.
5 Roll out 175 g (6 oz) of the pastry into a rectangle 15 x 30 cm (6 x 12 inch). Place on a baking sheet, prick with a fork and bake at 200°C (400°F) mark 6 for about 15 minutes. Cool.
6 Place the cooked pastry on a baking sheet. Top with the pepper strips, crumbled ricotta, goat's cheese then the spinach, making an indentation along the centre. Fill with the mushroom mixture.
7 Thinly roll out 225 g (8 oz) pastry, large enough to wrap around the filling with some to tuck under the base. Brush with egg. Use the remaining pastry and trimmings for a lattice pattern over the top. Glaze with egg and chill until ready to cook.
8 Bake at 220°C (425°F) mark 7 for about 35-40 minutes.

TOMATO AND GRUYERE PIE

PREPARATION TIME 15 minutes, plus pastry
COOKING TIME 40 minutes
FREEZING Not suitable

SERVES 4

580 CALS/SERVING

- *30 ml (2 tbsp) vegetable oil*
- *75 g (3 oz) onion, peeled and finely chopped*
- *225 g (8 oz) firm, green tomatoes, thinly sliced*
- *125 g (4 oz) Gruyère cheese, grated*
- *45 ml (3 tbsp) chopped fresh basil*
- *90 ml (6 tbsp) mayonnaise*
- *salt and pepper*
- *225 g (8 oz) Puff Pastry (see page 75)*
- *beaten egg, to glaze*

1 Heat the oil in a frying pan and gently sauté the onion for 2-3 minutes. Add the tomatoes and cook for 3-4 minutes or until beginning to soften, stirring occasionally.
2 Transfer to a bowl and stir in the cheese, basil, mayonnaise and seasoning.
3 Thinly roll out the puff pastry, cut out a 25 cm (10 inch) round and place on a baking sheet. Spread the tomato mixture over the centre to within 1 cm (½ inch) of the edge. Brush the pastry edge with beaten egg.
4 Bake at 180°C (350°F) mark 4 for 30-35 minutes until golden. Serve the pie hot or warm.

SUMMER COUSCOUS

PREPARATION TIME 30 minutes
FREEZING Not suitable
♡ ◴

SERVES 6

230 CALS/SERVING

- *225 g (8 oz) couscous*
- *6 spring onions, roughly chopped*
- *3 tomatoes, diced*
- *6 sun-dried tomatoes in oil, drained and chopped*
- *125 g (4 oz) pitted black olives*
- *30 ml (2 tbsp) chopped fresh mint*
- *15 ml (1 tbsp) each chopped fresh coriander and chopped fresh parsley*
- *2-3 garlic cloves, peeled and crushed*
- *45 ml (3 tbsp) olive oil*
- *juice of 1 lemon*
- *salt and pepper*

1 Put the couscous in a large bowl and pour in 600 ml (1 pint) cold water. Leave to soak for 15-20 minutes or until all the liquid has been absorbed.
2 Mix all the remaining ingredients into the couscous with plenty of seasoning.

TIP

This dish can be prepared the day before, if wished. Cover and chill.

SUMMER RISOTTO

PREPARATION TIME 5 minutes
COOKING TIME About 25 minutes
FREEZING Not suitable
♡ ◴

SERVES 4

- *225 g (8 oz) mixed, wild long-grain rice*
- *350 ml (12 fl oz) vegetable stock*
- *15 ml (1 tbsp) oil (from sun-dried tomatoes, if using)*
- *1 garlic clove, peeled and crushed*
- *350 g (12 oz) tomatoes, diced*

350-375 CALS/SERVING

- *4 sun-dried tomatoes in oil, drained and diced (optional)*
- *700 g (1½ lb) mixed blanched French beans, broad beans, mangetout, peas and asparagus*
- *12 pitted black olives, halved*
- *salt and pepper*

1 Cook the rice in the stock for about 20 minutes or until all the liquid has been absorbed and the rice is tender.
2 Heat the oil in a large non-stick frying pan or wok. Add the garlic and cook, stirring for 1-2 minutes.
3 Add the tomatoes and rice. Cook, stirring, over a gentle heat for 3-4 minutes. Stir in the blanched vegetables and olives. Increase the heat and cook for 1 minute, stirring, until piping hot. Season well and serve immediately.

TURKISH AUBERGINES

PREPARATION TIME 15 minutes, plus chilling
COOKING TIME 1½ hours
FREEZING Not suitable

SERVES 6

- *6 small aubergines*
- *200 ml (7 fl oz) olive oil*
- *450 g (1 lb) onions, peeled and finely sliced*
- *3 garlic cloves, peeled and crushed*
- *400 g (14 oz) can tomatoes, drained, or 450 g (1 lb) fresh tomatoes, skinned and chopped*

365 CALS/SERVING

- *60 ml (4 tbsp) chopped fresh parsley*
- *3.75 ml (¾ tsp) ground allspice*
- *salt and pepper*
- *5 ml (1 tsp) sugar*
- *30 ml (2 tbsp) lemon juice*
- *fresh parsley, to garnish*

1 Halve the aubergines lengthways. Scoop out the flesh and reserve. Leave a substantial shell so that they do not disintegrate.
2 Heat 45 ml (3 tbsp) of the olive oil in a saucepan, add the onions and garlic and fry gently for about 15 minutes or until the onions are soft but not coloured. Add the tomatoes, reserved aubergine flesh, chopped parsley and allspice. Season with salt and pepper. Simmer gently for about 20 minutes or until the mixture has reduced.
3 Spoon the tomato mixture into the aubergine halves and place them side by side in a shallow ovenproof dish. They should fit quite closely together.
4 Mix the remaining oil with 150 ml (5 fl oz) water, the sugar and lemon juice. Season with salt and pepper. Pour the mixture around the aubergines, cover and cook in the oven at 150°C (300°F) mark 2 for about 1 hour or until tender.
5 When cooked, remove from the oven, uncover and leave to cool for 1 hour. Chill in the refrigerator for at least 2 hours before serving garnished with parsley.

VEGETABLE KEBABS WITH MANGO SAUCE AND TROPICAL RICE

PREPARATION TIME 20 minutes
COOKING TIME 20-25 minutes
FREEZING Not suitable

SERVES 4

- *5 ml (1 tsp) sesame or sunflower oil*
- *1 small onion, peeled and very finely chopped*
- *1 garlic clove, peeled and finely chopped*
- *45 ml (3 tbsp) mango chutney*
- *45 ml (3 tbsp) tomato purée*
- *grated rind and juice of 1 lime*
- *150 ml (5 fl oz) natural yogurt*

386 CALS/SERVING

- *salt and pepper*
- *8 shallots or baby onions, peeled*
- *2 courgettes, trimmed*
- *225 g (8 oz) button mushrooms*
- *175 g (6 oz) baby sweetcorn*
- *225 g (8 oz) basmati or long-grain rice*
- *40 g (1½ oz) creamed coconut, diced*

1 Heat the oil in a non-stick saucepan, add the onion and garlic and cook for about 5 minutes until softened. Remove from the heat and stir in the mango chutney, tomato purée, half the lime juice and the yogurt. Season with salt and pepper.
2 Put the shallots in a saucepan of boiling water, return to the boil, then drain well. Cut the courgettes into 2.5 cm (1 inch) pieces. Thread the shallots, courgettes, mushrooms and sweetcorn alternately onto eight skewers.
3 Arrange the skewers on a foil-lined grill pan. Brush the kebabs with mango sauce and cook under a hot grill for 10-15 minutes, turning frequently, until golden brown.
4 Meanwhile, cook the rice for 10-12 minutes until cooked. Drain, then add the lime rind and remaining lime juice and the coconut. Stir until the coconut has melted.
5 Gently heat the remaining sauce but do not allow to boil. Pour into a serving bowl. Serve the kebabs with the tropical rice and mango sauce.

BROAD BEANS IN HERBED LEMON CREAM

PREPARATION TIME 20 minutes
COOKING TIME About 20 minutes
FREEZING Not suitable

SERVES 4-6

- *50 g (2 oz) butter*
- *2 garlic cloves, peeled and chopped*
- *4 shallots, peeled and finely chopped*
- *450 g (1 lb) fresh baby broad beans, shelled*
- *150 ml (5 fl oz) vegetable stock*
- *200 ml (7 fl oz) double cream*

385-260 CALS/SERVING

- *30 ml (2 tbsp) chopped fresh chervil or chives*
- *30 ml (2 tbsp) chopped fresh parsley*
- *grated rind of 1 lemon*
- *salt and pepper*

1 Melt the butter in a saucepan, add the garlic and shallots and cook gently for 3 minutes. Stir in the beans and stock. Bring to the boil, cover and simmer gently for 12-15 minutes, until the beans are tender.
2 Strain, reserving the liquid. Place the cooking liquid in a blender or food processor with 90 ml (4 tbsp) beans and blend to a purée, gradually adding the cream to make a smooth sauce.
3 Return the mixture to the pan. Add the beans, herbs and lemon rind and season with salt and pepper to taste. Reheat gently and serve hot.

VARIATION Omit the lemon rind and sprinkle with crisp, crumbled bacon just before serving.

TIP

Tender, fresh baby broad beans are best for this dish, or use frozen baby beans and skin them, if necessary, before cooking.

OKRA WITH APRICOTS

PREPARATION TIME 10 minutes
COOKING TIME 35-40 minutes
FREEZING Not suitable

SERVES 4

250 CALS/SERVING

- *450 g (1 lb) small okra*
- *juice of ½ orange*
- *60 ml (4 tbsp) olive oil*
- *1 onion, peeled and thinly sliced*
- *400 g (14 oz) can tomatoes*
- *30 ml (2 tbsp) tomato purée*
- *125 g (4 oz) no-soak dried apricots, cut into thick shreds*
- *salt and pepper*
- *30 ml (2 tbsp) chopped fresh basil*
- *orange rind strips and orange slices, to garnish*

1 Place the okra in a bowl, pour over the orange juice, toss lightly and set aside.
2 Heat the oil in a large saucepan, add the onion and cook for 5 minutes until softened. Add the okra and orange juice, then add the tomatoes and break up slightly with a wooden spoon.
3 Stir in the tomato purée and the apricots and season with salt and pepper to taste. Cover the pan and cook gently for 30-35 minutes until the okra and apricots are tender and the sauce thickened.
4 Stir in the basil and serve hot, garnished with orange rind strips and orange slices.

BAKED ARTICHOKES

PREPARATION TIME 10 minutes
COOKING TIME 45-50 minutes
FREEZING Not suitable
♡

SERVES 6

110 CALS/SERVING

- *6 small globe artichokes*
- *salt and pepper*
- *90 ml (6 tbsp) extra-virgin olive oil*
- *lemon slices and chervil or parsley sprigs, to garnish*

1 Trim the artichoke stalks close to the base. Bring a large saucepan of salted water to the boil.
2 Add the artichokes. Simmer, covered, for 30 minutes or until you can pull away a base leaf easily.
3 Drain the artichokes and refresh under cold water, then halve them lengthways. With a small spoon, remove the 'hairy' choke.
4 Place the artichokes cut side uppermost on a baking sheet. Drizzle with olive oil and season with salt and pepper. Bake at 200°C (400°F) mark 6 for about 15-20 minutes. Serve garnished with lemon slices and herbs.

VARIATION The artichokes can be grilled instead of baked. Grill for 20 minutes, basting occasionally with olive oil.

PAN-FRIED TOMATOES

PREPARATION TIME 8 minutes
COOKING TIME 3 minutes
FREEZING Not suitable

SERVES 4

240 CALS/SERVING

- *450 g (1 lb) plum tomatoes, thickly sliced*
- *rock salt and pepper*
- *100 ml (3½ fl oz) olive oil*
- *2 garlic cloves, peeled and sliced*
- *30 ml (2 tbsp) capers, drained and rinsed*
- *30 ml (2 tbsp) chopped fresh parsley*

1 Season the tomatoes with salt and pepper.
2 Heat the olive oil with the garlic in a large sauté pan. Fry the tomatoes for 1 minute only on each side. Using draining spoons, remove to a shallow serving dish.
3 Add the capers and parsley to the pan. Heat for 1 minute, stirring, then pour the contents of the pan over the tomatoes. Serve at once.

TIP
This dish also makes a refreshing starter served warm or cold with toasted ciabatta bread and goats' cheese.

STIR-FRIED SUMMER VEGETABLES

PREPARATION TIME 15 minutes
COOKING TIME 5 minutes
FREEZING Not suitable
♡ ◴

SERVES 4-6

- *30 ml (2 tbsp) sunflower oil*
- *2.5 cm (1 inch) piece fresh root ginger, peeled and finely chopped (optional)*
- *1 garlic clove, peeled and finely chopped*
- *175 g (6 oz) baby carrots, trimmed*
- *125 g (4 oz) baby French beans, topped and tailed*
- *175 g (6 oz) baby courgettes (with flowers, if possible), halved lengthways*
- *125 g (4 oz) mangetout or sugar snap peas*

195-130 CALS/SERVING

- *125 g (4 oz) baby sweetcorn, halved diagonally*
- *3-4 spring onions, shredded*
- *175 g (6 oz) bean sprouts, rinsed*
- *30 ml (2 tbsp) light soy sauce*
- *salt and pepper*
- *5-10 ml (1-2 tsp) sesame oil*
- *coriander sprigs, to garnish*

SAUCE

- *45 ml (3 tbsp) sherry*
- *45 ml (3 tbsp) light soy sauce*
- *5 ml (1 tsp) clear honey*

1 To make the sauce, simply mix the sherry, soy sauce and honey together in a small jug; set aside.
2 Heat the oil in a wok or large frying pan and add the ginger and garlic to flavour the oil. When the oil is very hot, add the carrots and French beans and fry, turning constantly, for 2-3 minutes.
3 Add the courgettes, mangetout or sugar snaps, sweetcorn, spring onions and bean sprouts, together with the soy sauce. Stir-fry for 2 minutes.
4 Taste and season with salt and pepper if necessary. Sprinkle with the sesame oil. Serve immediately, garnished with coriander sprigs and accompanied by the sauce.

VARIATION To serve the stir-fry as a main course, include rice noodles or egg noodles. Cook according to the packet instructions until almost tender. Drain. Add to the stir-fry and cook,

ROASTED TOMATOES, PEPPERS AND COURGETTES

PREPARATION TIME 10 minutes, plus cooling
COOKING TIME 45 minutes
FREEZING Not suitable

SERVES 4

215 CALS/SERVING

- *225 g (8 oz) aubergine, cut into large chunks*
- *350 g (12 oz) courgettes, cut into large chunks*
- *1 red pepper, deseeded and cut into chunks*
- *1 yellow pepper, deseeded and cut into chunks*
- *225 g (8 oz) tomatoes, halved*
- *6 garlic cloves, peeled*
- *75 ml (5 tbsp) olive oil*
- *rock salt and pepper*
- *1 lemon*

1 Place all the vegetables in a large roasting tin in a single layer. Sprinkle the olive oil over them and season generously with plenty of rock salt.
2 Roast at 200°C (400°F) mark 6 for about 45 minutes or until tender and well browned, turning once during cooking.
3 Cool for 30 minutes in the tin and then squeeze over lemon juice to taste and adjust the seasoning. Lift the vegetables onto serving plates or into one large bowl. Serve straight away or leave to cool.

TIP

For a delicious light lunch, serve the roasted vegetables with this toasted treat – thickly slice a crusty loaf and rub each slice with a garlic clove. Toast lightly on both sides. Spread the toast thickly on both sides with pesto sauce or tapenade (olive paste), then top with slices of mozzarella, Emmental or goats' cheese. Place the slices under the grill until the cheese just begins to melt.

NEW POTATO AND DILL SALAD

PREPARATION TIME 5 minutes
COOKING TIME 15 minutes
FREEZING Not suitable

SERVES 6

215 CALS/SERVING

- *900 g (2 lb) baby new potatoes*
- *salt and pepper*
- *60 ml (4 tbsp) Greek natural yogurt*
- *60 ml (4 tbsp) mayonnaise*
- *20 ml (4 tsp) wholegrain mustard*
- *5 ml (1 tsp) lemon juice*
- *60 ml (4 tbsp) chopped fresh dill or 2.5 ml (½ tsp) dried*

1 Scrub the new potatoes. Boil them in salted water for 10-15 minutes or until tender.
2 Meanwhile, mix the remaining ingredients together and season with salt and pepper.
3 Drain the potatoes and leave to cool for 5 minutes, then mix with the dressing while still warm. Serve warm or cover and chill.

VARIATION Turn this into an inexpensive supper dish by mixing in some smoked salmon scraps, available from fishmongers.

MIXED HERB SALAD

PREPARATION TIME 15 minutes
FREEZING Not suitable
♡ ◴

SERVES 4

- *selection of seasonal fresh herb leaves, such as rocket, sorrel, lamb's lettuce, dandelion, enough for 4 people*
- *handful of chervil sprigs*
- *handful of parsley sprigs*
- *a few flowers, such as sweet violets and marigolds, if available*

100 CALS/SERVING

- *2.5 ml (½ tsp) dry mustard powder*
- *5 ml (1 tsp) clear honey*
- *30 ml (2 tbsp) lemon juice*
- *2.5 ml (½ tsp) paprika*
- *30 ml (2 tbsp) sunflower oil*
- *15 ml (1 tbsp) walnut oil*
- *salt and pepper*

1 Wash and drain the salad leaves. Gently pat dry with absorbent kitchen paper. Shred them roughly by hand. Place them in a serving bowl with the chervil and parsley sprigs. Scatter the flowers, if using, over the top. Cover tightly and refrigerate until ready to dress the salad.
2 Blend the mustard powder with the honey until smooth. Add the lemon juice, paprika, sunflower and walnut oils and seasoning. Mix well.
3 Dress the salad about 10 minutes before serving.

MIXED LEAF, ORANGE AND STRAWBERRY SALAD

PREPARATION TIME 20 minutes
FREEZING Not suitable
♡ ◴

SERVES 6

- *1 small frisée lettuce*
- *1 bunch watercress*
- *3 large oranges*
- *225 g (8 oz) strawberries*
- *1 large ripe avocado*
- *45 ml (3 tbsp) olive oil*

150 CALS/SERVING

- *5 ml (1 tsp) white wine vinegar*
- *5 ml (1 tsp) Dijon mustard*
- *salt and pepper*

1 Wash and dry the frisée and watercress, removing any coarse or discoloured stalks or leaves. Tear into small pieces and place in a large serving bowl.
2 Peel the oranges and slice into the serving bowl. Wash, hull and slice the strawberries; halve, peel and slice the avocado and place both in the bowl.
3 To make the dressing, whisk together the olive oil, wine vinegar and Dijon mustard. Season with salt and pepper to taste. Pour the dressing over the prepared salad. Toss well and serve.

TOMATO AND RED ONION SALAD

PREPARATION TIME 10 minutes, plus marinating
FREEZING Not suitable
♡ ◴

SERVES 6

- *700 g (1½ lb) mixed tomatoes, halved*
- *1 large red onion, peeled and finely chopped*

120 CALS/SERVING

- *60 ml (4 tbsp) olive oil*
- *20 ml (4 tsp) balsamic vinegar*
- *salt and pepper*

1 Combine the tomatoes and onion.
2 Whisk together the remaining ingredients and season with salt and pepper. Pour over the tomatoes, toss well and leave to marinate for at least 20 minutes before serving.

CUCUMBER AND WATERCRESS SALAD

PREPARATION TIME 10 minutes, plus chilling
FREEZING Not suitable
♡ ◷

SERVES 6

- *30 ml (2 tbsp) white wine vinegar*
- *5 ml (1 tsp) sugar*
- *15 ml (1 tbsp) olive oil*
- *20 ml (4 tsp) lemon juice*
- *salt and pepper*
- *1 cucumber, weighing about 350 g (12 oz) and cut into matchsticks*

70 CALS/SERVING

- *small bunch spring onions, sliced*
- *25 g (1 oz) chopped walnuts*
- *1 bunch watercress, divided into sprigs*

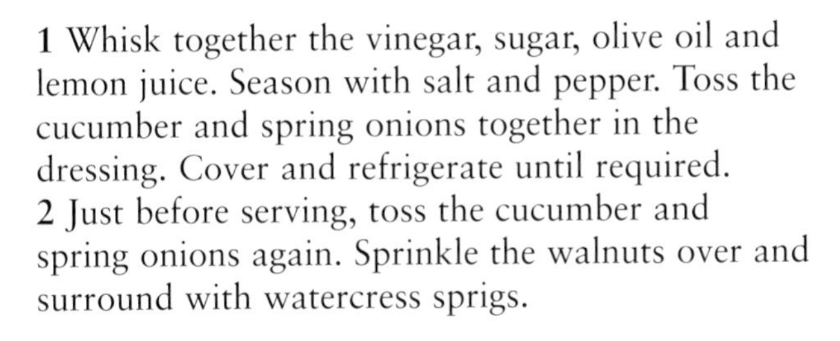
1 Whisk together the vinegar, sugar, olive oil and lemon juice. Season with salt and pepper. Toss the cucumber and spring onions together in the dressing. Cover and refrigerate until required.
2 Just before serving, toss the cucumber and spring onions again. Sprinkle the walnuts over and surround with watercress sprigs.

TIP

This is a useful salad for preparing in advance and assembling at the last minute. Store the watercress sprigs in a polythene bag in the refrigerator.

FETA CHEESE AND OLIVE SALAD

PREPARATION TIME 15 minutes
FREEZING Not suitable
◷

SERVES 2

- *225 g (8 oz) tomatoes*
- *½ large cucumber*
- *125 g (4 oz) feta cheese*
- *1 onion, peeled and thinly sliced*
- *50 g (2 oz) pitted black olives*
- *chopped fresh herbs, to garnish*

430 CALS/SERVING

DRESSING

- *45 ml (3 tbsp) olive oil*
- *15-30 ml (1-2 tbsp) lemon juice*
- *15-30 ml (1-2 tbsp) chopped fresh herbs*
- *pinch of sugar*
- *salt and pepper*
- *crusty bread, to accompany*

1 Whisk the dressing ingredients together in a jug or shake together in a screw-topped jar.
2 Cut the tomatoes into bite-sized chunks, discarding the cores. Cut the cucumber and feta cheese into bite-sized chunks.
3 Put the tomatoes, cucumber and onion in a large bowl, add the olives and toss the ingredients together with your hands. Pour over the dressing and toss gently to mix, then scatter the feta cheese over the top. Serve as soon as possible, garnished with chopped fresh herbs and accompanied with slices of crusty bread.

ARTICHOKE AND ASPARAGUS SALAD

PREPARATION TIME 25 minutes, plus marinating
COOKING TIME 30-45 minutes
FREEZING Not suitable
♡

SERVES 6

- *6 small, young or 3 large, firm artichokes*
- *salt and pepper*
- *350 g (12 oz) asparagus*
- *100 ml (3½ fl oz) olive oil*
- *30 ml (2 tbsp) orange juice*
- *30 ml (2 tbsp) chopped fresh herbs such as basil, lemon thyme and marjoram or 10 ml (2 tsp) dried*

200 CALS/SERVING

- *1 bunch radishes*
- *175 g (6 oz) mixed black and green olives, with stones*
- *fresh basil, to garnish (optional)*

1 If using small, young artichokes, trim each stalk to within 4 cm (1½ inches) of the head and plunge into a large saucepan of boiling, salted water. Cover and simmer for 20-25 minutes or until tender when the base is pierced with the tip of a sharp knife. If using large artichokes, break and pull off the stalks. Snip off the sharp tips of the leaves. Cook in a large pan of boiling, salted water for 35-45 minutes, weighing them down with a heatproof plate or small lid to keep them completely submerged. They are cooked when a central leaf can be pulled out easily.
2 Drain the artichokes and plunge into cold water, then drain and pat dry on absorbent kitchen paper. Leave to cool. When completely cold, quarter each large artichoke and, using a teaspoon, very carefully scoop out the hairy choke at the base.
3 Trim any tough or woody stalks from the asparagus, cut into 5 cm (2 inch) lengths and plunge into boiling, salted water for 8-10 minutes or until tender but still crisp. Plunge into cold water and drain.
4 In a large bowl, whisk together the olive oil, orange juice, chopped herbs and salt and pepper to taste. Add the cooked vegetables and toss well to coat.
5 Trim the radishes; halve or quarter, if necessary. Place the olives in a polythene bag and lightly 'crack' with a rolling pin. Add the radishes and olives to the vegetables and toss lightly. Cover and leave to marinate in the refrigerator for 4 hours or overnight. (The flavour is better the longer you leave it.)
6 Allow the salad to come to room temperature for about 2 hours. Serve garnished with extra basil sprigs, if wished.

AVOCADO AND CHICK-PEA SALAD

PREPARATION TIME 15 minutes
FREEZING Not suitable
◴

SERVES 4

- *45 ml (3 tbsp) lemon juice*
- *50 g (2 oz) fromage frais*
- *125 ml (4 fl oz) milk*
- *30 ml (2 tbsp) chopped fresh chives or parsley*
- *salt and pepper*
- *1 avocado*
- *450 g (1 lb) fresh young spinach, finely shredded*

330 CALS/SERVING

- *125 g (4 oz) radicchio lettuce, finely shredded*
- *430 g (15 oz) can chick-peas, drained and rinsed*
- *1 slice of wholemeal bread, toasted and cubed*
- *2 eggs, hard-boiled and chopped*
- *paprika*

1 To make the dressing, place 30 ml (2 tbsp) of the lemon juice, the fromage frais and milk in a bowl and whisk until smooth. Add the herbs and salt and pepper to taste. Set aside.
2 Peel the avocado, discard the stone and dice the flesh. Coat with the remaining lemon juice to prevent discoloration.
3 Mix together the spinach and radicchio leaves and arrange on a large serving platter. Scatter the avocado, chick-peas, toast cubes and eggs on top and sprinkle over a little paprika.
4 To serve, spoon a little of the dressing over the salad. Serve the remaining dressing separately.

MINTED VEGETABLE SALAD

PREPARATION TIME 20 minutes
COOKING TIME 4 minutes
FREEZING Not suitable
♡ ◴

SERVES 6 | 145 CALS/SERVING

- *45 ml (3 tbsp) chopped fresh mint*
- *50 ml (2 fl oz) olive oil*
- *30 ml (2 tbsp) white wine vinegar*
- *grated rind of 1 lemon*
- *5 ml (1 tsp) Dijon mustard*
- *5 ml (1 tsp) caster sugar*
- *225 g (8 oz) shelled*
- *175 g (6 oz) shelled broad beans*
- *salt and pepper*
- *225 g (8 oz) courgettes, thickly sliced*
- *175 g (6 oz) runner beans, trimmed and sliced*
- *1 bunch spring onions, finely chopped*
- *fresh mint leaves, to garnish*

1 Whisk together the mint, olive oil, vinegar, lemon rind, mustard and sugar, then set aside.
2 Place the peas and beans in a saucepan of boiling, salted water. Return to the boil, cook for 3 minutes, add the courgettes and runner beans and boil for a further 1 minute, or until just tender. Drain well, then refresh under cold water so that they retain their colour.
3 Toss the vegetables with the spring onions in the prepared mint dressing, adjust the seasoning and serve warm or cold, garnished with mint.

TIP

Don't toss the dressing in until the last minute or you'll find that the vegetables will lose their bright colour.

BERRY COMPOTE

PREPARATION TIME 15 minutes
COOKING TIME 5 minutes
FREEZING Not suitable
♡ ◷

SERVES 6

95 CALS/SERVING

- *50 g (2 oz) granulated sugar*
- *225 g (8 oz) blackcurrants, prepared*
- *450 g (1 lb) redcurrants, prepared*
- *pared rind and juice of 1 orange*
- *30 ml (2 tbsp) clear honey*
- *350 g (12 oz) strawberries, hulled*

1 Dissolve the sugar in 150 ml (5 fl oz) water. Bring to the boil and bubble for 1 minute.
2 Add the prepared currants with the pared orange rind and simmer for about 1 minute only until the fruits are just beginning to soften. Immediately remove from the heat and pour into a heatproof bowl. Stir in the honey and leave to cool.
3 Mix in the strained orange juice, cover the bowl and chill well in the refrigerator.
4 Just before serving, thinly slice the strawberries and stir gently into the compote.

NOTE With 50 g (2 oz) sugar the compote will be quite tart – add more sugar to taste.

STRAWBERRY MILLE FEUILLES

PREPARATION TIME 1 hour, plus chilling and cooling
COOKING TIME 15 minutes
FREEZING Suitable for the pastry
❄

SERVES 6-8

425-320 CALS/SERVING

- *225 g (8 oz) Puff Pastry (see page 75)*
- *50 g (2 oz) raspberries*
- *30 ml (2 tbsp) redcurrant jelly*
- *350 g (12 oz) strawberries, hulled and halved*
- *150 ml (5 fl oz) double cream, whipped*
- *strawberry leaves, to decorate*

CREME PATISSIERE

- *300 ml (10 fl oz) milk*
- *1 vanilla pod, split*
- *3 egg yolks*
- *75 g (3 oz) caster sugar*
- *30 ml (2 tbsp) cornflour*
- *15 g (½ oz) butter*

1 Roll out the pastry to a 23 x 30 cm (9 x 12 inch) rectangle. Transfer to a dampened baking tray, prick the pastry all over with a fork and chill for 15 minutes. Bake at 220°C (425°F) mark 7 for 10-12 minutes until golden brown. Trim the edges, then cut widthways into three equal strips. Turn the strips over, return to the oven and bake for 5 minutes more. Cool on a wire rack.
2 To make the crème pâtissière, heat the milk with the vanilla pod in a heavy-based saucepan until almost boiling, then remove from the heat and leave to infuse for 30 minutes.
3 Whisk together the egg yolks and sugar until frothy, then whisk in the cornflour. Strain in the milk and whisk again. Return this mixture to the pan and cook over a low heat, stirring all the time, until boiling and thickened. Remove from the heat and beat in the butter. Cover the surface of the sauce with clingfilm and leave to cool.
4 Meanwhile, purée the raspberries in a blender and place in a saucepan with the redcurrant jelly. Place over a low heat and stir until the jelly has melted. Leave to cool, stirring occasionally, then stir in one third of the strawberries. When the crème pâtissière is cold, fold in the cream.
5 When ready to serve, spread the crème pâtissière over two strips of the pastry and carefully arrange half of the plain strawberries on top of each. Lay one strip on top of the other, then top with the final layer of pastry and spoon the fruit mixture on top. Decorate and serve at once.

STRAWBERRY CHEESECAKE

PREPARATION TIME 25 minutes, plus cooling
COOKING TIME 50 minutes
FREEZING Suitable (stage 3)
❄

SERVES 8

- *50 g (2 oz) butter or margarine*
- *75 g (3 oz) plain flour*
- *25 g (1 oz) porridge oats*
- *75 g (3 oz) caster sugar*
- *700 g (1½ lb) natural cottage cheese*
- *2 eggs*

245 CALS/SERVING

- *grated rind of 1 lemon*
- *60 ml (4 tbsp) natural yogurt*
- *225 g (8 oz) fresh strawberries, hulled*

1 Grease and base-line a 20 cm (8 inch) loose-based round cake tin. Put the fat in a saucepan and heat until melted, then stir in the flour, oats and 25 g (1 oz) of the sugar. Stir until well mixed, then press into the base of the cake tin. Bake at 180°C (350°F) mark 4 for 10 minutes.

2 Meanwhile, rub the cottage cheese through a sieve into a bowl. Beat the eggs, then beat into the cottage cheese. Add the lemon rind and the remaining 50 g (2 oz) caster sugar and mix well together.

3 Pour the mixture into the cake tin. Return to the oven and bake for 20 minutes. Spoon the yogurt over the cheesecake and bake for a further 20 minutes. Leave to cool in the tin for 3-4 hours.

4 When cold, carefully remove the cheesecake from the tin. Slice most of the strawberries and arrange, with the remaining whole berries, on top of the cheesecake before serving.

TIP

The texture of a cooked cheesecake almost seems to improve with standing. Make and cook the day before and store, undecorated, in the refrigerator overnight. Remove from the refrigerator an hour before serving, to allow the cheesecake to return to room temperature.

SUMMER PUDDING

PREPARATION TIME 35 minutes, plus chilling
COOKING TIME 5 minutes
FREEZING Suitable
♡ ❄

SERVES 6-8

- *450 g (1 lb) raspberries*
- *225 g (8 oz) redcurrants, prepared*
- *225 g (8 oz) blackcurrants, prepared*
- *75 g (3 oz) caster sugar*
- *8 large slices white bread, 5 mm (1/4 inch) thick*
- *redcurrant sprigs and lemon balm or mint leaves, to decorate*

180-135 CALS/SERVING

1 Place the raspberries in a saucepan, with the red and black currants, sugar and 45 ml (3 tbsp) water. Bring to a gentle simmer over a low heat, then cook gently for 3-4 minutes until the juices begin to run. Set aside.
2 Remove the crusts from the bread slices, then cut a round of bread from one slice to fit the base of a 1.5 litre (2½ pint) pudding basin. Cut the remaining slices in half lengthways.
3 Arrange the bread slices around the side of the pudding basin, overlapping them slightly at the bottom, so they fit neatly and tightly together. Position the round of bread to cover the base.
4 Spoon 100 ml (3½ fl oz) of the fruit juice into a jug. Spoon the remaining fruit and its juice into the bread-lined basin. Cover completely with the remaining bread slices, trimming to fit.
5 Cover the pudding with a saucer, that fits just inside the top of the pudding basin, then set a 2 kg (4 lb) weight on the saucer. Chill overnight.
6 To serve the pudding, invert onto a serving plate, spoon the reserved juice over the pudding and decorate with redcurrant sprigs and lemon balm or mint sprigs.

NOTE Choose a good quality close-textured large

RASPBERRY FOOL

PREPARATION TIME 10 minutes, plus chilling
FREEZING Not suitable
♡

SERVES 4

- *450 g (1 lb) raspberries*
- *25 g (1 oz) caster sugar*
- *300 ml (10 fl oz) very low-fat fromage frais*
- *raspberry leaves, to decorate (optional)*

95 CALS/SERVING

1 Reserve a few raspberries for decoration. Put the rest with the sugar in a blender or food processor and process to form a purée.
2 Turn the raspberry purée into a bowl, then gently swirl in the fromage frais to make a marbled effect. Divide the mixture between 4 individual serving dishes.
3 Chill in the refrigerator for about 2 hours before serving. Serve decorated with the reserved raspberries and raspberry leaves, if wished.

NOTE Using low-fat fromage frais makes this delicious fool surprisingly light in calories.

VARIATIONS Strawberry fool can be made in exactly the same way as the above recipe, simply substituting strawberries for the raspberries. For a mixed soft fruit fool, use an equal weight of raspberries and strawberries. Don't forget to reserve a little of the fruit for decoration.

CHERRY BRULEES

PREPARATION TIME 15 minutes, plus chilling
COOKING TIME 40-45 minutes
FREEZING Not suitable

SERVES 8

- *350 g (12 oz) fresh cherries*
- *15 ml (1 tbsp) kirsch*
- *4 egg yolks*
- *50 g (2 oz) caster sugar*

395 CALS/SERVING

- *450 ml (15 fl oz) double cream*
- *125 g (4 oz) granulated sugar*

1 Stone the cherries, reserving eight with stems for decoration. Pour the kirsch over the remaining pitted cherries.
2 Whisk together the egg yolks and caster sugar until they have thickened and lightened in colour. Pour in the cream, stirring. Place in a heavy-based saucepan. Cook over a low heat, stirring continuously, until the mixture thickens to the consistency of double cream. This will take about 10 minutes. Do not boil.
3 Divide the soaked cherries among 8 ramekins or heatproof cups. Strain over the custard mixture.
4 Bake at 150°C (300°F) mark 2 for 30-35 minutes or until very lightly set. Cool and refrigerate until firm.
5 Place the granulated sugar in a small, heavy-based saucepan. Heat gently until the sugar dissolves and turns a golden caramel colour. Place a reserved cherry on each ramekin. Pour a thin layer of the caramel over each one. Chill, uncovered, for about 1 hour but not more than 6 hours before serving.

TIP
Cherry stoners are available from all good kitchen equipment shops. This inexpensive tool not only saves time but removes the stone with very little damage.

GOOSEBERRY MOUSSE

PREPARATION TIME 25 minutes, plus setting
COOKING TIME 15 minutes
FREEZING Not suitable
♡

SERVES 4

- *15 ml (1 tbsp) powdered gelatine*
- *450 g (1 lb) gooseberries, trimmed*
- *50 g (2 oz) caster sugar*

130 CALS/SERVING

- *150 ml (5 fl oz) natural yogurt*
- *a few drops of green food colouring (optional)*
- *fresh mint sprigs, to decorate*

1 In a small bowl, sprinkle the gelatine over 60 ml (4 tbsp) cold water. Put the gooseberries in a saucepan with 30 ml (2 tbsp) water. Bring to the boil, reduce the heat, cover and simmer for 15 minutes until the fruit is tender. If very juicy, drain off the cooking liquid and reserve. Stir in the sponged gelatine and stir well. Cool slightly.
2 Put the gooseberries and sugar in a blender or food processor and process to form a purée.
3 Push the purée through a nylon sieve into a measuring jug to remove the seeds. If necessary, make up to 450 ml (15 fl oz) with reserved juice.
4 When the gooseberry mixture is beginning to set, fold in the yogurt. Add a few drops of green food colouring if wished.
5 Pour the mousse into 4 individual serving dishes or one large dish. Put in the refrigerator to set. Serve decorated with sprigs of fresh mint.

POACHED APRICOTS

PREPARATION TIME 10 minutes, plus chilling
COOKING TIME 10 minutes
FREEZING Not suitable
♡

SERVES 6

100 CALS/SERVING

- *18 apricots, about 700 g (1½ lb) total weight*
- *1 cinnamon stick*
- *50 g (2 oz) caster sugar*
- *300 ml (10 fl oz) white wine*
- *1 vanilla pod*
- *15 ml (1 tbsp) brandy*

1 Halve and stone the apricots, if wished.
2 Cut the cinnamon stick lengthways and place in a saucepan with the sugar, wine, vanilla pod and 225 ml (8 fl oz) water.
3 Heat gently until the sugar dissolves. Bring to the boil and bubble for 2-3 minutes. Add the apricots and brandy and reduce to gentle simmer. Poach the fruit for 5-6 minutes or until just tender.
4 Pour into a heatproof glass bowl and leave to cool completely. Cover and chill in the refrigerator before serving.

NOTE When chilling the dish, make sure that the apricots are covered in syrup so that they don't discolour.

TIP
This recipe makes plenty of syrup for the apricots; if you don't serve it all, freeze the remainder and use as a base for a fruit salad.

GOLDEN NECTARINE TART

PREPARATION TIME 20 minutes, plus cooling
COOKING TIME 1 hour 20 minutes
FREEZING Suitable (stage 2)
❄

SERVES 8

500 CALS/SERVING

PATE SUCREE
- *125 g (4 oz) butter*
- *225 g (8 oz) white plain flour*
- *125 g (4 oz) caster sugar*
- *1 whole egg plus 1 egg yolk, beaten together*

FILLING
- *15 g (½ oz) fresh white breadcrumbs*
- *6 ripe nectarines or peaches, about 700 g (1½ lb) total weight*
- *2 whole eggs plus 1 egg yolk*
- *200 ml (7 fl oz) double cream*
- *40 g (1½ oz) icing sugar*
- *30 ml (2 tbsp) brandy*
- *1.25 ml (¼ tsp) freshly grated nutmeg*
- *90 ml (6 tbsp) apricot jam*

1 Make the pâte sucrée following the instructions on page 76.
2 Roll out the pâte sucrée carefully and use to line a 2.5 cm (1 inch) deep, 27.5 x 19.5 cm (10¾ x 7¾ inch) loose-based flan tin. Bake blind (see page 75) until set and lightly browned, then leave to cool.
3 Scatter the breadcrumbs evenly over the pastry base. Halve and stone the nectarines and arrange cut side down in the flan case.
4 Whisk together the two eggs, egg yolk, double cream, icing sugar, brandy and nutmeg. Pour the mixture around the nectarines.
5 Bake at 180°C (350°F) mark 4 for about 50 minutes or until just set. Flash under a hot grill to brown, then set aside to cool.
6 Warm the jam with 15 ml (1 tbsp) water to make a glaze. Sieve, then brush the glaze over the flan. Leave to set. Store in a cool place until ready to serve – not more than 6 hours.

VARIATION For an alternative dessert with fewer calories (215 per serving), simply place the nectarines in a shallow ovenproof dish. Pour the whisked egg mixture over and bake as above. Peaches can also be used but remove the skin first as it can be tough when cooked.

GRILLED PEACHES WITH CHOCOLATE AND MARZIPAN

PREPARATION TIME 10 minutes
COOKING TIME 5 minutes
FREEZING Not suitable

SERVES 4

- *4 ripe peaches*
- *150 ml (5 fl oz) double cream*
- *125 g (4 oz) plain chocolate, broken into pieces*
- *1 lime*
- *50 g (2 oz) marzipan, chopped into small pieces*

445 CALS/SERVING

- *30 ml (2 tbsp) icing sugar*
- *pouring cream, to serve*
- *mint sprigs, to decorate*

1 Halve the peaches and remove the stones. Arrange the peaches, cut-side up, in a shallow flameproof dish.
2 Pour the cream into a saucepan. Bring just to the boil, then add the chocolate and stir until smooth.
3 Pare thin strips of rind from the lime using a citrus zester; set aside. Squeeze 10 ml (2 tsp) juice from the lime and add to the chocolate sauce. Sprinkle a further 10 ml (2 tsp) over the peaches.
4 Divide the marzipan between the peach halves. Drizzle a little of the chocolate sauce over the peaches and pour the remainder into the dish.
5 Sift the icing sugar over the peaches and grill for about 5 minutes until the peaches and marzipan are lightly coloured.
6 Transfer to warmed serving plates and scatter with the pared lime rind. Pour a little cream onto the sauce. Serve decorated with mint sprigs and accompanied by pouring cream.

VARIATION Use ripe nectarines or pears in place of the peaches. You may need to take a thin slice off the rounded sides of the pears so they sit flat.

ICED ORANGE AND LEMON TERRINE WITH BURNT SUGAR SAUCE

PREPARATION TIME 25 minutes, plus chilling and freezing
COOKING TIME 8 minutes (sauce)
FREEZING Suitable (stage 3)
❄

SERVES 6

- *4 egg yolks*
- *30 ml (2 tbsp) caster sugar*
- *300 ml (10 fl oz) whipping cream*
- *finely grated rind and juice of 1 large orange*
- *finely grated rind and juice of 1 lemon*

375 CALS/SERVING

- *mandarin or orange segments, to decorate*

SAUCE

- *125 g (4 oz) caster sugar*
- *juice of ½ lemon*
- *pinch of salt*
- *150 ml (5 fl oz) single cream*

1 Using an electric whisk, whisk together the egg yolks and sugar for 5 minutes or until pale and thick.
2 Lightly whip the cream until it just holds its shape. Fold it into the egg mixture, along with all the orange and lemon juice and rind. The mixture will become quite liquid.
3 Line a 1.1 litre (2 pint) terrine or loaf tin with clingfilm. Pour in the mixture and freeze for 3 hours or overnight.
4 To make the sauce, put the sugar, plus 100 ml (3½ fl oz) water and the lemon juice in a heavy-based saucepan. Place over a medium heat for about 3 minutes, until the sugar has dissolved. Do not stir. Increase the heat and cook for 5 minutes, until the sugar is a light caramel colour. Add the salt and, off the heat, stir in the cream. Chill for 3 hours or overnight.
5 Briefly dip the tin in hot water, then invert the terrine onto a serving plate. Remove the clingfilm and slice the terrine with a hot knife. Serve with the burnt sugar sauce and decorate with mandarin segments.

NOTE The young, the elderly, pregnant women and people with immune-deficiency diseases should not eat raw eggs, due to the possible risk of salmonella.

FROZEN STRAWBERRY ICE

PREPARATION TIME 10 minutes, plus freezing
FREEZING Suitable
♡ ❄

SERVES 6

- *450 g (1 lb) strawberries, hulled*
- *150 ml (5 fl oz) low-fat or low-calorie ice cream, slightly softened*
- *150 ml (5 fl oz) low-fat bio natural yogurt*

110 CALS/SERVING

- *15 ml (1 tbsp) framboise or cassis liqueur*
- *2 egg whites*
- *2 oranges*
- *strawberry leaves, to decorate*

1 In a blender or food processor, blend 225 g (8 oz) of the strawberries, the ice cream, yogurt and liqueur until smooth.
2 In a clean, dry bowl, whisk the egg whites until they just form soft peaks. Fold them into the strawberry mixture. Divide the mixture among 6 individual ramekins and freeze for at least 4 hours, or preferably overnight.
3 Slice the remaining strawberries into a bowl. Add the juice of the oranges, cover and marinate for about 1 hour.
4 To serve, dip the outside of the ramekins into warm water for a few seconds and turn out onto serving plates. Leave at room temperature for about 10 minutes to soften a little before serving with the marinated strawberries. Decorate with strawberry leaves.

MELON ICE

PREPARATION TIME 20 minutes, plus marinating and freezing
FREEZING Suitable (stage 3)
❄

SERVES 6-8

- *450 ml (16 fl oz) double cream*
- *75 g (3 oz) caster sugar*
- *700 g (1½ lb) ripe orange-fleshed melon, such as charentais or cantaloupe, halved and deseeded*
- *250 ml (9 fl oz) sweet wine, such as Moscatel de Valencia, or a light sugar syrup*

465-350 CALS/SERVING

- *1 ripe ogen or galia melon, halved and deseeded*
- *ginger biscuits, to serve*
- *fresh mint sprigs, to decorate*

1 Gently heat the cream and sugar until the sugar dissolves, stirring, then set aside to cool.
2 Place the 700 g (1½ lb) melon flesh in a blender or food processor with half the wine. Blend until smooth, then sieve to remove any coarse fibres.
3 Mix the sweetened cream with the purée. Pour into a freezerproof container. Freeze for 2½-3 hours, then stir to break down any ice crystals. Repeat this process twice, then leave to freeze for at least 2 hours until firm.
4 Scoop out the ogen or galia melon flesh with a melon baller and place in serving bowls. Pour a little of the remaining wine over each serving. Marinate in the refrigerator for about 1 hour.
5 To serve, scoop the melon ice into balls and serve with the marinated melon and ginger biscuits. Decorate with mint sprigs.

TIP
Although any freezerproof container is suitable for holding water ices or ice creams, a shallow one speeds up the freezing process.

LEMON SPONGE WITH KIRSCH AND FRESH CURRANTS

PREPARATION TIME 25 minutes, plus cooling
COOKING TIME About 30 minutes
FREEZING Suitable (stage 4)
♡ ❄

SERVES 8-10

- *3 eggs*
- *125 g (4 oz) caster sugar*
- *finely grated rind of 1 lemon*
- *75 g (3 oz) plain flour*
- *25 g (1 oz) unsalted butter, melted*
- *125 g (4 oz) red-currants, prepared*
- *125 g (4 oz) white-currants, prepared*
- *60 ml (4 tbsp) kirsch*
- *15 ml (1 tbsp) lemon juice*
- *icing sugar, for dusting*
- *sprigs of lemon balm or mint, to decorate, (optional)*

170-140 CALS/SERVING

TIP

This delicious syrup-topped ring cake can double up as a summer dessert, served with crème fraîche.

1 Grease the base of a 1.7 litre (3 pint) ring tin. Dust the sides of the tin with flour, shaking out the excess.

2 Put the eggs, 75 g (3 oz) sugar and the lemon rind in a large heatproof bowl set over a pan of hot water. Whisk until pale and creamy and thick enough to leave a trail on the surface when the whisk is lifted.

3 Remove from the heat and whisk until cool. Sift half the flour over the mixture and fold in with a large metal spoon. Pour half the butter around the edge of the mixture and fold in. Gradually fold in the remaining butter and flour.

4 Pour into the prepared tin and bake at 190°C (375°F) mark 5 for about 25 minutes until just firm to the touch. Loosen the edges of the tin, then turn the sponge onto a wire rack to cool.

5 Dissolve the remaining sugar in 75 ml (3 fl oz) water in a small saucepan. Bring to the boil and boil for 1 minute. Add the red and white currants and simmer for 1 minute. Stir in the kirsch and lemon juice. Leave to cool. Place the sponge on a serving plate and pour over the currant syrup.

6 Just before serving, dust the sponge with icing sugar and decorate with sprigs of lemon balm or mint, if wished.

RASPBERRY MOUSSE GÂTEAU

PREPARATION TIME 1½ hours, plus chilling
COOKING TIME 30-35 minutes
FREEZING Suitable (stage 6)

❄

SERVES 6-8

- *175 g (6 oz) shelled hazelnuts*
- *4 eggs*
- *125 g (4 oz) light muscovado sugar*
- *125 g (4 oz) white plain flour*
- *2.5 ml (½ tsp) baking powder*
- *25 g (1 oz) butter, melted and cooled*

845-630 CALS/SERVING

FILLING

- *450 g (1 lb) raspberries*
- *1 egg, separated*
- *25 g (1 oz) caster sugar*
- *7.5 ml (1½ tsp) powdered gelatine*
- *450 ml (15 fl oz) double cream*
- *150 ml (5 fl oz) Greek-style yogurt*

1 Grease and base-line a 20 cm (8 inch) round cake tin. Spread out the hazelnuts on a baking sheet and grill until browned. Leave to cool, then roughly chop 25 g (1 oz) and set aside. Finely grind the remaining nuts.
2 Whisk the eggs and muscovado sugar in a large bowl over a saucepan of barely simmering water until the mixture is thick and pale and will hold a trail. Remove the bowl from the heat and whisk for a further 3 minutes. Sift the flour and baking powder together and fold into the mixture alternately with the ground hazelnuts and butter.
3 Spread the mixture in the prepared tin and bake at 180°C (350°F) mark 4 for 30-35 minutes until risen and firm to the touch. Turn out, remove the paper and cool on a wire rack.
4 To make the mousse filling, rub half the raspberries through a sieve. Whisk the egg yolk, sugar and raspberry purée in a large bowl over a pan of barely simmering water until the mixture is thick and foamy and will hold a trail. Remove the bowl from the heat and whisk until cold.
5 Sprinkle the gelatine over 30 ml (2 tbsp) water in a small heatproof bowl and leave to soak, then stand the bowl in a pan of hot water until the gelatine is dissolved. Whip 50 ml (2 fl oz) cream and fold into the raspberry mixture. Gently stir in the gelatine. Whisk the egg white until holding soft peaks, then fold into the mixture.
6 Line a 20 cm (8 inch) spring-release cake tin with clingfilm. Cut the hazelnut cake into three rounds and trim to a 20 cm (8 inch) diameter. Place one sponge round in the base of the tin. Whip 150 ml (5 fl oz) cream and fold in the yogurt, then spread over the cake. Scatter over one third of the reserved raspberries and cover with a second sponge round. Spoon on the mousse, scatter over another third of the raspberries and cover with the remaining sponge. Press down gently. Chill for 2 hours or until set.
7 Transfer to a plate. Whip the remaining cream and spoon mounds onto the cake. Scatter raspberries and chopped nuts in the middle.

CHOCOLATE ROULADE

PREPARATION TIME 30 minutes, plus cooling
COOKING TIME 25 minutes
FREEZING Suitable (undecorated)

❄

SERVES 6-8

- *60 ml (4 tbsp) cocoa powder*
- *150 ml (5 fl oz) milk*
- *4 eggs, separated*
- *125 g (4 oz) caster sugar*
- *150 ml (5 fl oz) double cream*

330-250 CALS/SERVING

- *150 ml (5 fl oz) Greek yogurt*
- *strawberries and grated chocolate, to decorate*

1 Grease and line a 20 x 30 cm (8 x 12 inch) Swiss roll tin. Mix the cocoa powder and milk in a small saucepan and heat gently until the cocoa powder has dissolved. Leave to cool.
2 Whisk the egg yolks and sugar together until pale and fluffy. Whisk the cooled milk mixture into the egg yolk mixture.
3 Whisk the egg whites until stiff, then fold into the cocoa mixture. Spread the mixture evenly into the prepared tin and bake in the oven at 180°C (350°F) mark 4 for about 20 minutes until the sponge has risen and is just firm to the touch.
4 Turn out onto a sheet of greaseproof paper and cover with a warm, damp tea towel to prevent the sponge from drying out. Leave for 20 minutes.
5 Meanwhile, whip the cream until quite stiff, then stir in the yogurt. Spread over the sponge, reserving half for decorating, and then roll it up carefully. Do not roll it up too tightly and do not worry if it cracks slightly. Decorate with cream, strawberries and chocolate. Serve chilled.

APRICOT JAM

PREPARATION TIME 20 minutes
COOKING TIME About 40 minutes
FREEZING Not suitable

MAKES ABOUT 3 KG (6½ LB)
- *1.8 kg (4 lb) apricots*
- *juice of 1 lemon*

40 CALS/15 ML (1 TBSP)
- *1.8 kg (4 lb) preserving sugar*
- *knob of butter*

1 Halve the apricots and remove the stones. Crack a few of the apricot stones with a weight, nutcracker or mallet. Take out the kernels and blanch them in boiling water for 1 minute, then drain.
2 Put the apricots, lemon juice, apricot kernels and 450 ml (15 fl oz) water in a preserving pan and simmer for about 15 minutes or until the fruit is soft and the contents of the pan are well reduced.
3 Take the pan off the heat and add the sugar, stirring until it dissolves. Add the butter and boil rapidly for about 15 minutes or until setting point is reached (see page 77).
4 Remove any scum with a slotted spoon, then pot and cover in the usual way (see page 77).

BERRY JAM

PREPARATION TIME 15 minutes
COOKING TIME 10 minutes
FREEZING Not suitable

MAKES ABOUT 1.8 KG (4 LB)
- *1 kg (2¼ lb) prepared strawberries*

35 CALS/15 ML (1 TBSP)
- *1 kg (2¼ lb) preserving sugar*
- *knob of butter*

1 Place the strawberries in a 4.5 litre (8 pint) heavy-based saucepan. Crush with a wooden spoon, then add the preserving sugar and heat gently until the sugar dissolves.
2 Add the butter and bring to a full, rolling boil. Boil for 4 minutes, then pot and cover in the usual way (see page 77).

SUMMER PICKLE

PREPARATION TIME 25 minutes, plus marinating
COOKING TIME about 8 minutes
FREEZING Not suitable

MAKES 450 G (1 LB)
- *225 g (8 oz) each celery, carrots, cucumber, red peppers and red onions*
- *125 g (4 oz) each green beans, baby sweetcorn and button mushrooms*
- *600 ml (1 pint) distilled malt vinegar*
- *6 allspice berries*
- *6 black peppercorns*
- *1 mace blade*

15 CALS/15 ML (1 TBSP)
- *1 bay leaf*
- *2 cloves*
- *pinch of powdered saffron or turmeric*
- *30 ml (2 tbsp) chopped dill*
- *90 ml (6 tbsp) light soft brown sugar*
- *salt and pepper*
- *125 g (4 oz) cherry tomatoes*
- *90 ml (6 tbsp) walnut oil*

1 Thickly slice the celery. Peel and thinly slice the carrots. Halve the cucumber lengthways and thickly slice. Deseed the peppers and cut into similar-sized pieces. Trim the onions, leaving the root intact, and cut into 8 'wedges' each. Top and tail the green beans and corn; trim the mushrooms.
2 Combine all the ingredients, except the cherry tomatoes and walnut oil, in a preserving pan or large saucepan. Bring to the boil and simmer, stirring gently, for 5 minutes.

3 Stir in the cherry tomatoes and walnut oil, then transfer to a non-metallic bowl. Cool, cover with a plate and leave to marinate overnight.
4 Pot and cover in the usual way (see page 77).

BRANDY-SOAKED CHERRIES

PREPARATION TIME 15 minutes
COOKING TIME 10 minutes
FREEZING Not suitable

MAKES 450 G (1 LB)
- *450 g (1 lb) cherries*
- *125 g (4 oz) sugar*
- *1 cinnamon stick*

35 CALS/25 G (1 OZ)
- *about 150 ml (5 fl oz) brandy*

1 Prick the whole cherries all over with a darning needle. Place the sugar in a saucepan with 150 ml (5 fl oz) water and heat gently until the sugar dissolves. Add the cherries and cinnamon stick and simmer very gently for 4-5 minutes.
2 Strain the cherries, reserving the liquid. Reheat the liquid with the brandy and boil for 3-4 minutes.
3 Place the cherries in a 600 ml (1 pint) sterilized jar and pour in the liquid until the cherries are completely covered. Cover with a lid or cork and store in the refrigerator for up to 2 months.

VARIATION Add a few orange or lemon slices to the jar, if wished.

MANGOADE

PREPARATION TIME 20 minutes, plus cooling

SERVES 4-6

150-100 CALS/SERVING

- *450 g (1 lb) ripe mango flesh, coarsely chopped*
- *50 g (2 oz) sugar, or to taste*
- *450 ml (15 fl oz) sparkling mineral water*
- *5 ml (1 tsp) grated orange rind*
- *450 ml (15 fl oz) orange juice*
- *ice cubes*
- *lime slices and rose petals, to decorate*

1 Purée most of the mango in a blender or food processor. Keep the rest on one side.
2 Combine the sugar, water and orange rind in a saucepan and heat, stirring, until the sugar dissolves. Cool, then add to the mango with the orange juice.
3 Serve on ice, in tall glasses, with the remaining mango and a slice of lime. Add a few rose petals, if wished, removing the white 'heels' first.

SUMMER PUNCH

PREPARATION TIME 5 minutes, plus chilling

SERVES 18-20

135-125 CALS/SERVING

- *3 bottles medium white wine, chilled*
- *¾ bottle dry sherry*
- *60 ml (4 tbsp) Grand Marnier or orange liqueur*
- *two 1 litre (1¾ pint) bottles tonic water*
- *crushed ice*
- *cucumber slices, apple slices and fresh mint sprigs, to decorate*

1 Mix the wine, sherry and liqueur in one or more jugs and chill for about 2 hours.
2 To serve, add the tonic and crushed ice. Decorate with the cucumber and apple slices and mint sprigs.

TIP

For a refreshing berry milkshake for two, place 400 g (14 oz) mixed soft fruits in a blender with 400 ml (14 fl oz) milk and purée until smooth. Sieve, then add sugar to taste. Chill well before serving.

APRICOT FLIP

PREPARATION TIME 20 minutes, plus chilling

SERVES 2

170 CALS/SERVING

- *400 g (14 oz) can of apricots in natural juice, drained*
- *150 g (5 oz) apricot yogurt*
- *10 ml (2 tsp) clear honey*
- *grated rind and juice of 2 oranges*

1 Purée the apricots in a blender or food processor until smooth.
2 Add the yogurt, honey and the juice from the oranges and purée for a further minute. Chill in the refrigerator.
3 Serve decorated with grated orange rind.

TROPICAL FRUIT CRUSH

PREPARATION TIME 15 minutes, plus chilling

SERVES 8-10

240-195 CALS/SERVING

- *600 ml (1 pint) orange juice, chilled*
- *2.4 litres (4 pints) grape juice, chilled*
- *1 litre (1¾ pints) tropical fruit juice, chilled*
- *1.8 litres (3 pints) sparkling mineral water, chilled*
- *selection of prepared fresh fruit, such as kiwi fruit, strawberries, lemon slices, raspberries and grapes*
- *ice cubes*
- *star fruit slices, to decorate (optional)*

1 Mix all the chilled liquids together in a large bowl just before you are ready to serve. Float all the prepared fruit on the top.
2 Ladle the drink into large wine glasses, and drop an ice cube or two into each glass. Decorate each glass with a slice of star fruit, if liked.

VARIATION If available, fresh fruit and basil leaves can be scattered over for decoration.

REDCURRANT RUM

PREPARATION TIME 30 minutes, plus standing and chilling

SERVES 16

200 CALS/SERVING

- *900 g (2 lb) redcurrants*
- *350 g (12 oz) caster sugar*
- *1 vanilla pod*
- *about 1 bottle white rum*
- *borage flowers, to decorate (optional)*

1 String and wash the redcurrants. Drain well.
2 Place them in a clean jar, add the sugar and vanilla pod. Top up with the rum.
3 Seal the jar with a rustproof lid and shake to mix. Leave in a cool, dark place for at least a week, and no longer than three months, shaking occasionally.
4 To use, remove the vanilla pod, chill the drink and serve straight or pour over ice and top up with sparkling mineral water. Decorate with borage flowers, if wished.

BASIC RECIPES

Making your own stocks and pastry will give recipes that extra depth of flavour, while homemade mayonnaise and bread will give everyday meals a culinary lift.

VEGETABLE STOCK

PREPARATION TIME 15 minutes
COOKING TIME 1¾ hours
FREEZING Suitable

MAKES 1.1 LITRES (2 PINTS)

- *30 ml (2 tbsp) vegetable oil*
- *1 onion, peeled and finely chopped*
- *1 carrot, peeled and diced*
- *50 g (2 oz) turnip, peeled and diced*
- *50 g (2 oz) parsnip, peeled and diced*
- *4 celery sticks, chopped*
- *vegetable trimmings, such as celery tops, cabbage leaves, mushroom peelings, tomato skins*
- *1 bouquet garni*
- *6 black peppercorns*
- *a little salt*

1 Heat the oil in a saucepan, add the onion and fry gently for about 5 minutes until lightly coloured.
2 Add the other vegetables to the pan with the trimmings and 1.7 litres (3 pints) water. Add the bouquet garni and peppercorns. Season with salt.
3 Bring to the boil, partially cover and simmer for 1½ hours, skimming occasionally.
4 Strain the stock and leave to cool. Cover and store in the refrigerator. Use within 1-2 days.

BEEF STOCK

PREPARATION TIME 15 minutes,
COOKING TIME 4½-5½ hours
FREEZING Suitable

MAKES 900 ML (1½ PINTS)

- *450 g (1 lb) shin of beef, cut into pieces*
- *450 g (1 lb) marrow bones or knuckle of veal, chopped*
- *1 bouquet garni*
- *1 onion, peeled and sliced*
- *1 carrot, peeled and sliced*
- *1 celery stick, sliced*
- *2.5 ml (½ tsp) salt*

1 To give a good flavour and colour, brown the meat and bones in the oven before using them. Place in a roasting tin and cook at 220°C (425°F) mark 7 for 30-40 minutes until well browned.
2 Put the bones and meat in a saucepan with 1.7 litres (3 pints) water, the bouquet garni, vegetables and salt. Bring to the boil and remove any scum.
3 Partially cover and simmer for 4-5 hours.
4 Strain and, when cold, remove all traces of fat.

CHICKEN STOCK

PREPARATION TIME 15 minutes
COOKING TIME 2-3 hours
FREEZING Suitable

MAKES 1.1 LITRES (2 PINTS)

- *1 chicken carcass, bones and trimmings from a roast chicken*
- *1 onion, peeled and sliced*
- *1 carrot, peeled and sliced*
- *1 celery stick, sliced*
- *1 bouquet garni*
- *1 bay leaf*
- *salt*

1 Break up the chicken carcass and put in a large saucepan with any skin and meat attached, plus other bones and trimmings.
2 Add 1.7 litres (3 pints) water, the onion, carrot, celery, bouquet garni, bay leaf and a little salt. Bring to the boil, then skim.
3 Partially cover and simmer for 2-3 hours.
4 Strain and, when cold, remove all traces of fat.

FISH STOCK

PREPARATION TIME 10 minutes
COOKING TIME 20 minutes
FREEZING Suitable

MAKES 900 ML (1½ PINTS)

- *450-750 g (1-1½ lb) fish bones and trimmings*
- *salt*
- *1 bouquet garni*
- *1 onion, peeled and sliced*

1 Put the fish bones and trimmings into a saucepan, cover with 900 ml (1½ pints) water and add a little salt. Bring to the boil, then skim.
2 Reduce the heat and add the bouquet garni and

onion. Cover and simmer for 20 minutes.
3 Strain and leave to cool. Use on the same day, or store in the refrigerator for not more than 2 days.

SHORTCRUST PASTRY

PREPARATION TIME 10 minutes, plus resting
FREEZING Suitable

For shortcrust pastry, the proportion of flour to fat is 2:1, or twice the quantity. Therefore, for a recipe using quantities of shortcrust pastry other than 225 g (8 oz), simply use half the quantity of fat to the flour weight specified.

MAKES 225 G (8 OZ)
- *225 g (8 oz) white plain flour*
- *pinch of salt*

175 CALS/25 G (1 OZ)
- *125 g (4 oz) butter or margarine, chilled and diced*

1 Mix flour and salt together in a bowl. Add the fat to the flour. Using your fingertips, rub the fat lightly into the flour until the mixture resembles fine breadcrumbs.
2 Add 45-60 ml (3-4 tbsp) chilled water, sprinkling it evenly over the surface.
3 Stir in with a round-bladed knife until the mixture begins to stick together in large lumps. Collect the dough mixture together to form a ball.
4 Knead lightly for a few seconds to give a firm, smooth dough; do not overhandle the dough. Wrap in clingfilm or greaseproof paper and rest in the refrigerator for about 30 minutes.
5 To roll out the pastry, sprinkle a very little flour on a work surface and the rolling pin (not on the pastry) and roll out the dough evenly in one direction only, turning it occasionally. The usual thickness is 3 mm (1/8 inch). Do not pull or stretch the pastry.

VARIATION ***Walnut Shortcrust Pastry*** Follow the recipe for Shortcrust Pastry, stirring in 40 g (1½ oz) very finely chopped, shelled walnuts before adding the water.

BAKING BLIND

If a recipe for a flan or tart instructs you to bake blind, it means that you should partially or completely bake the pastry case before filling. To bake blind, first prick the pastry base with a fork, then line with a large piece of greaseproof paper or foil. Fill with ceramic baking beans or dried pulses. Small cases don't need lining – just prick with a fork.

For partially baked cases, bake at 200°C (400°F) mark 6 for 10-15 minutes until the case looks 'set'. Carefully remove the paper or foil and the beans and bake for a further 5 minutes until the base is firm to the touch and lightly coloured.

For completely baked cases, return to the oven for about 15 minutes until firm and golden brown.

PUFF PASTRY

PREPARATION TIME 40 minutes, plus resting
FREEZING Suitable

The richest of all the pastries, puff requires patience, practice and very light handling. Whenever possible it should be made the day before use. It is not practical to make in a quantity with less than 450 g (1 lb) flour weight. This quantity is equivalent to two 375 g (13 oz) packets.

MAKES 450 G (1 LB)
- *450 g (1 lb) strong plain flour*
- *pinch of salt*
- *450 g (1 lb) butter or margarine, chilled*

270 CALS/25 G (1 OZ)
- *15 ml (1 tbsp) lemon juice*

1 Mix the flour and salt together. Cut off 50 g (2 oz) of the butter and flatten the remaining butter with a rolling pin to a slab 2 cm (3/4 inch) thick.
2 Cut the 50 g (2 oz) butter into small pieces, add to the flour and rub in. Using a round-bladed knife, stir in the lemon juice and about 300 ml (10 fl oz) chilled water to make a soft, elastic dough.
3 Quickly knead the dough until smooth and shape into a round. Cut through half the depth in the shape of a cross. Open out to form a star.
4 Roll out, keeping the centre four times as thick as the flaps. Place the slab of butter in the centre.
5 Fold the flaps envelope-style and press gently with a rolling pin. Roll out to a rectangle measuring about 40 x 20 cm (16 x 8 inches).
6 Fold bottom third up and top third down, keeping the edges straight. Seal edges. Wrap in greaseproof paper and rest in the refrigerator for 30 minutes.
7 Put the pastry on a lightly floured work surface with the folded edges to the sides, then repeat the rolling, folding and resting sequence 5 times.

PATE SUCREE

PREPARATION TIME 10 minutes, plus resting
FREEZING Suitable

Pâte Sucrée is the classic French rich short pastry used for sweet flans.

MAKES 125 G (4 OZ)

255 CALS/25 G (1 OZ)

- *125 g (4 oz) white plain flour*
- *pinch of salt*
- *50 g (2 oz) butter (at room temperature)*
- *2 egg yolks*
- *50 g (2 oz) caster sugar*

1 Sift the flour and salt onto a work surface. Make a well in the centre and add the butter, egg yolks and sugar.
2 Using the fingertips of one hand, pinch and work the sugar, butter and egg yolks together until well blended.
3 Gradually work in all the flour to bind the mixture together. Knead lightly until smooth, then wrap the pastry in clingfilm and leave to rest in a cool place for at least 30 minutes. Roll out as for Shortcrust Pastry (see page 75).

SWEET FLAN PASTRY

PREPARATION TIME 10 minutes, plus resting
FREEZING Suitable

This is made by the same method as shortcrust pastry, but beaten egg is used instead of water.

MAKES 125 G (4 OZ)

250 CALS/25 G (1 OZ)

- *125 g (4 oz) white plain flour*
- *pinch of salt*
- *75g (3 oz) butter or margarine, chilled and diced*
- *5 ml (1 tsp) caster sugar*
- *1 egg, beaten*

1 Sift the flour and salt into a bowl. Rub in the fat until the mixture resembles fine breadcrumbs. Stir in the sugar.
2 Add the egg, stirring with a round-bladed knife until the ingredients begin to stick together.
3 With one hand, form into a firm, smooth dough. Wrap the pastry in clingfilm and rest in a cool place for at least 30 minutes. Roll out as for Shortcrust Pastry (see page 75).

WHOLEMEAL BREAD

PREPARATION TIME 30 minutes, plus rising
COOKING TIME 35 minutes
FREEZING Suitable

MAKES 1 LOAF

1700 CALS/LOAF

- *15 g (½ oz) fresh yeast or 7 g sachet (1½ tsp) fast-action dried yeast*
- *150 ml (5 fl oz) tepid milk*
- *450 g (1 lb) wholemeal plain flour*
- *5 ml (1 tsp) salt*
- *5 ml (1 tsp) caster sugar*
- *25 g (1 oz) butter or margarine*
- *beaten egg, water or milk for glazing*

1 If using fresh yeast, blend with the milk. Mix the flour, salt and sugar in a bowl, and stir in the fast-action dried yeast if using. Rub in the butter. Make a well in centre and pour in the yeast liquid or milk and about 175 ml (6 fl oz) tepid water. Mix to a soft dough.
2 Turn out the dough onto a lightly floured surface and knead for about 10 minutes until smooth and elastic. If using fresh yeast, place in an oiled bowl and cover with oiled clingfilm. Leave to rise until doubled in size and sponge-like.
3 Knock the risen dough down, then knead again on a lightly floured surface for 3-4 minutes until smooth. Flatten the dough to an oblong the length of a 900 g (2 lb) loaf tin but three times as wide. Fold in three, turn over, then place in the lightly greased tin.
4 Cover the dough with oiled clingfilm and leave to rise in a warm place for about 45 minutes, or until the dough has risen to the rim of the tin.
5 Brush with beaten egg, water or milk to glaze. Bake at 220° C (425° F) mark 7 for 20 minutes. Reduce the temperature to 180° C (350° F) mark 4 and remove the bread from the tin. Bake for a further 15 minutes. To test, tap the bottom crust; the bread should sound hollow. Cool on wire rack.

NOTE Dough made with fast-action dried yeast only requires one rising. Glazing with beaten egg produces a deep golden shiny finish; brushing with water gives a crisp crust; milk produces a soft, golden crust.

VARIATION *Soft White Bread:* Use strong white plain flour with 200 ml (7 fl oz) tepid milk and 75 ml (3 fl oz) tepid water.

MAYONNAISE

PREPARATION TIME 10-15 minutes
FREEZING Not suitable

MAKES 150 ML (5 FL OZ)

140 CALS/15 ML (1 TBSP)

- *1 egg yolk*
- *2.5 ml (½ tsp) mustard powder or 5 ml (1 tsp) Dijon mustard*
- *2.5 ml (½ tsp) salt*
- *1.25 ml (¼ tsp) pepper*
- *15 ml (1 tbsp) white wine vinegar or lemon juice*
- *about 150 ml (5 fl oz) oil*

1 Put the egg yolk in a bowl with the mustard, seasoning and 5 ml (1 tsp) of the vinegar or lemon juice. Mix thoroughly.
2 Add the oil drop by drop to begin with, then in a steady stream, whisking constantly, until the sauce is thick and smooth. If it becomes too thick, add a little more vinegar or lemon juice.
3 When all the oil has been added, add the remaining vinegar or lemon juice gradually and mix thoroughly. Store for up to 3 days in the refrigerator.
NOTE Never use eggs straight from the refrigerator as this may result in curdling.

PRESERVING TIPS

Making your own jams, jellies, chutneys and other preserves is one of the most satisfying ways of storing abundant seasonal fruit and vegetables. To achieve the best results, there are certain points about the process you should bear in mind.

PRESERVING EQUIPMENT

If you make a lot of preserves, it's worth investing in a proper preserving pan; the sloping sides help maintain a fast boil and reduce the chances of everything boiling over. Choose a pan made from stainless steel, tin-lined copper or lined aluminium. Don't use unlined aluminium.

If you don't have a preserving pan use a large heavy-based saucepan instead. Note that if you are using a saucepan rather than a preserving pan the preserve will take much longer to reach the setting point owing to the reduced surface area.

For jelly making, you will need a jelly bag for straining the juice from the cooked fruit. Although you can improvise with a large piece of muslin, a jelly bag is a worthwhile investment because it makes things easier. Whatever you use, it should be scalded with boiling water before use. If the jelly bag doesn't have a stand, suspend it from the legs of an upturned chair or stool.

TESTING FOR A SET

Jams, jellies, marmalades and conserves are cooked sufficiently when setting point is reached. There are various tests to determine this. Remove the pan from the heat while you are testing, to prevent overcooking.

Temperature test: The preserve is ready when the temperature registers 105°C (221°F) on a sugar thermometer.
Saucer test: Drop a spoonful of the preserve onto a chilled saucer and leave to cool. Push your finger through the jam; if the surface wrinkles, the preserve is ready.
Flake test: Using a wooden spoon, lift a little of the preserve out of the pan. Let it cool slightly then tip the spoon so that the preserve drops back into the pan; if the drips run together and fall from the spoon in a 'flake' rather than as drips, it is ready.

There is no accurate test for chutneys and pickles, because they are not cooked to a setting point. Instead, be guided by the consistency and cooking time specificed in the recipe; they are ready when the mixture is very thick.

POTTING PRESERVES

All preserves should be potted into scrupulously clean containers. Wash jars or bottles in really hot soapy water, rinse thoroughly, then dry in a warm oven. Stand them upside down on a clean tea towel until the preserve is ready. Aim to pour hot jam or marmalade into the jars while they are still warm, to reduce the chances of the glass cracking, and fill them almost to the top. If potting jam, jelly, marmalade or conserve, cover with a waxed disc while the preserve is piping hot or else completely cold, then seal with a dampened clear disc secured with an elastic band. If you seal while the preserve is warm, mould will grow on the surface. Chutneys and pickles are covered in the same way. For long-term storage, cover the jar with a screw top as well.

FREEZING

Freezing is an easy and convenient way to preserve fresh food, allowing you to save and store for later use the wealth of seasonal delicacies that are available fresh for only a short time of the year. Whether you freeze ingredients in their basic state or made up into complete dishes, you will find a well-stocked freezer an invaluable help for producing nutritious meals with the minimum of fuss - especially if you also own a microwave for rapid thawing and reheating.

TIPS FOR EFFICIENT FREEZING

• Freeze only food of the best quality. Never freeze food that looks blemished or old.
• Handle the food as little as possible.
• Never put any foods that are still slightly warm into the freezer, as a rise in temperature causes frosting up and deterioration of other foods will result.
• Never freeze more than one tenth of your freezer's capacity in any 24 hours, as this will also cause the internal temperature to rise.
• When freezing large quantities, use the fast-freeze option.
• Pack and seal food with care. If moisture or cold air is allowed to come into contact with the food it will begin to deteriorate. Cross flavouring might also occur.
• Be sure to wrap non-packaged foods well before freezing. Solid foods must be packaged tightly, with as little air as possible. Wrap items in foil or freezer film; ordinary clingfilm is not suitable for the freezer. Freezer film can also be used as a lining for acidic foods which should then be overwrapped in foil.
• Where possible use square containers to store food in the freezer; they stack better than round ones and therefore waste less space.
• Interleave any items of food that might otherwise stick together with pieces of greaseproof paper, polythene, foil or freezer film.
• When freezing liquids always leave room for expansion, as frozen liquid expands by about one-tenth of its volume and will push the lids off containers that have been overfilled.
• Freeze single and double portions for easy use.
• Keep you freezer as full as possible. If necessary add loaves of bread to fill up spaces. Empty spaces require more energy to keep cool.
• Make sure food is clearly labelled and dated. Always use up old stocks first. To help you do this it is a good idea to keep a freezer log book, adding items (with the date) as you freeze them and deleting them as they are consumed.
• Do not re-freeze food once it has been thawed, unless it has been subsequently cooked.
• Check your freezer is operating correctly with a freezer thermometer. It should read -18°C (0°F).

FREEZER STORAGE CHART

This chart is a guide to approximate maximum storage times for certain types of food. Always follow the manufacturer's instructions.

VEGETABLES
blanched vegetables (most types) 10-12 months
mushrooms and tomatoes 6-8 months
vegetable purées 6-8 months

FRUIT
fruit in syrup 9-12 months
open frozen fruit 6-8 months
fruit purées 6-8 months
fruit juice 4-6 months

FISH
white fish 6-8 months
oily fish 3-4 months
fish portions 3-4 months
shellfish 2-3 months

MEAT AND POULTRY
beef and lamb 4-6 months
pork and veal 4-6 months
offal 3-4 months
sliced bacon/other cured meat 2-3 months
ham and bacon joints 3-4 months
chicken and turkey 4-6 months
duck and goose 4-6 months
venison 4-6 months
rabbit and game 4-6 months
sausages, sausagemeat 2-3 months
minced beef 3-4 months

PREPARED FOOD
soups and sauces 3 months
stock 6 months
prepared meals 4-6 months
if highly seasoned 2-3 months
bread 2-3 months

pastries 3-4 months
cakes 4-6 months

DAIRY PRODUCE
cream 6-8 months
butter (salted) 3-4 months
cheese (hard) 4-6 months
cheese (soft) 3-4 months
ice cream, mousses etc 3-4 months

FREEZER EMERGENCIES

The most common freezer emergency is loss of power. This can be as a result of a power cut or someone inadvertently turning the freezer off. If there is a power cut, don't panic; if you leave the freezer door closed the food should stay frozen for about 30 hours (48 hours in a chest freezer). If possible, wrap the freezer with a blanket to increase insulation.

If you have advance warning of a power cut, turn on the fast-freeze switch, making sure the freezer is full to capacity. Towels or rolled newspaper can be used to fill any gaps.

Do not re-freeze any food you suspect may have begun to thaw.

FREEZING FRESH VEGETABLES

Vegetables can be very successfully frozen, but only if they are really fresh - no more than 12 hours after they were picked. Blanching the vegetables before freezing will help to preserve their colour, flavour and texture.

To blanch vegetables, bring a large pan of water to the boil and immerse the vegetables up to 450 g (1 lb) at a time. Bring back to the boil and keep the vegetables immersed for the required time - delicately textured or leafy vegetables such as spinach, mangetout and sliced courgettes will only need about 10 seconds, while firmer varieties such as broccoli and cauliflower florets, green beans and peas will need to be blanched for 1 minute. Root vegetables like carrots should be sliced and blanched for 2-3 minutes, while whole dense vegetables like globe artichokes and small beetroot need 4-5 minutes.

Once blanched, immediately remove the vegetables and plunge into a bowl of iced water. The blanching water can be used 6-7 times and the iced water refreshed with more ice as necessary. The vegetables can be put into a blanching basket for this part of the operation, but if you do not have one a suitable strainer or a large piece of muslin will do.

FREEZING FRESH FRUIT

First, check that the fruit you wish to freeze is properly ripe and in peak condition, free from any blemishes. Any overripe fruit should be puréed before freezing. With fruits such as apples you will have to cook them first before puréeing, but fruits such as peaches and raspberries can be puréed in their fresh form.

Before freezing the fruit, consider how it will eventually be used. Small fruits which do not need peeling are best frozen as they are; remove any stalks if necessary, and open freeze by spreading them on trays lined with non-stick paper, then transfer to polythene bags. They will not stick together, enabling small quantities to be removed as needed.

Firm fruits and any which have a tendency to discolour should be frozen in a syrup made with 450 g (1 lb) sugar to 1 litre (1¾ pints) water and the juice of 1 lemon. The fruits can be left whole, halved or sliced into the cool syrup as appropriate. For fruits such as grapefruit and pineapple omit the lemon juice and substitute any juice from the fruit.

THAWING FROZEN FOOD

Thawing must be done thoroughly and efficiently to ensure food is safe to eat.

- Never leave food to thaw in a warm environment; this is the ideal breeding ground for harmful bacteria. Instead, let the food thaw gradually in the refrigerator or in a cool larder.
- Cover food loosely while thawing.
- Make sure large items such as joints of meat are thoroughly thawed before cooking. The legs of poultry should be able to move freely.
- Dispose of any liquid which seeps from thawing meat and poultry. Do not allow it to come into contact with other food.
- Cook food as soon as possible after it is thawed.
- If thawing frozen food in a microwave, follow the manufacturer's instructions.
- Only use the microwave if you plan to eat or cook the food immediately.

INDEX